THREE TEAM PLAYS

This book is dedicated to the tens of thousands
of young people to whom we presented these plays,
with whom we shared workshops, and from
whom we learned so much.

Team Theatre Presents
Three Team Plays

John McArdle, *'Jacko'*

Frank McGuinness, *'Borderlands'*

Bernard Farrell, *'Then Moses met Marconi'*

Editor: Martin Drury

WOLFHOUND

Published 1988
WOLFHOUND PRESS
68 Mountjoy Square,
Dublin 1.

Performance Enquiries
Apply to individual authors at
TEAM Theatre Company,
4 Marlborough Place,
Dublin 1, who will direct enquiries to the relevant author.

This book is published with the assistance of The Arts Council (An Chomhairle Ealaíon), Dublin, Ireland.

British Library Cataloguing in Publication Data
Three Team plays.
   1. English drama — 20th century
   I. Drury, Martin   II. Farrell, Bernard.
Then Moses met Marconi   III. McGuinness,
Frank.   Borderlands   IV. McArdle, John.
Jacko
822'.914'08   PR1272

ISBN 0-86327-107-3

Cover design: Jan de Fouw
Typesetting: Redsetter Ltd.
Printed by Billings & Sons Ltd.

Contents

Introduction   7
Team Programmes 1975-87   14

Jacko by John McArdle
    Introduction   17
    The Play   19

Then Moses Met Marconi by Bernard Farrell
    Introduction   79
    The Play   83

Borderlands by Frank McGuinness
    Introduction   150
    The Play   153

Some Production Stills   193

The Workshops
    A General Note   201
    Jacko Workshops   202
    Moses Workshops   207
    Borderlands Workshops   216

SOME PRESS REACTIONS TO THE PLAYS

JACKO

"a monument of dramatic sensitivity . . . . McArdle unfolds the story meticulously and etches the sad ending with dignity and insight"
Irish Press

"a vivid and often compulsive documentary drama"
Evening Herald

"JACKO penetrated like a laser beam into the minds and hearts of those lucky enough to see it"   *Cork Examiner*

"simple in effect but large in concern . . . one of the most moving theatrical experiences I have had"   *Evening Echo*

THEN MOSES MET MARCONI

"highly amusing" *Evening Herald;* "very funny" *Irish Press;* "a very funny comedy" *The Irish Times;* "delectable comedy . . . thoroughly funny" *Evening Echo;* "brilliantly funny" *Limerick Leader.*

"Bernard Farrell's fast-moving satire will cheer up the gloomiest souls"   *Irish Independent*

"thoroughly exciting, theatrically fresh and modern"   *Southern Star*

BORDERLANDS

"This is fine theatre"   *The Irish Times*

"An interesting and stimulating piece which avoids cliche and pat answers"   *Sunday Tribune*

"Immediate, intimate, energetic . . . a provocative play, matched to the times we live"   *Theatre Ireland*

Introduction

THREE TEAM PLAYS

The plays in this volume were all written for performance to an audience of senior second-level students, aged between fifteen and eighteen years. However all three plays have been seen, enjoyed and much admired by adult audiences and indeed two of them have had major public tours on the Irish professional touring theatre circuit. This volume is intended for theatre companies, both professional and amateur, for teachers and youth leaders anxious to find new dramatic writing of appeal to young people, and for the ordinary reader who will find here three excellent plays about different aspects of contemporary Ireland.

Anyone in search of a new play, for a cast of six, has my full support if (s)he ignores this introduction and the notes at the back and goes straight for the texts to see 'if they can be put on by my group'. (S)he will not be disappointed. However, as the title THREE TEAM PLAYS suggests, there is a unity of purpose and a common impulse to the three plays, and it therefore seems worthwhile to record the context in which they were written and originally performed. To that end each play is prefaced by a short introduction and at the end of the volume there are extensive notes on the workshops which were designed to accompany each play when it was presented in schools. These notes will be of value to directors and actors involved in producing the plays as they seek to understand the texts better, and to teachers using the plays in a classroom context. The workshop notes contain descriptions of some drama games and exercises and indeed many drama-in-education approaches which TEAM uses and which should prove stimulating for directors, teachers, and youth leaders who use drama.

This book is published partly as a celebration of TEAM's years of service as Ireland's first full-time theatre-in-education company. In those years the company has forged a tradition of T.I.E. (theatre-in-education) and it is part of that tradition which this volume captures in print and photograph. Everyone in Ireland is 'on' for celebration but before it begins I anticipate and try to answer the question 'what exactly are we celebrating?'.

TEAM AND THE YOUNG ABBEY

TEAM was founded in September 1975 as an independent theatre-in-education company. The roots of the company, both in structure and inspiration, go back further however to the Young Abbey which was started in 1970 by Joe Dowling. In 1974 the Young Abbey was disbanded, chiefly because of lack of finance. Nevertheless a model of a new form of theatre had been established and the persistence of a few committed individuals saw to it that TEAM was founded the following year. In the thirteen years of its existence the company has developed enormous experience in T.I.E. and a considerable reputation throughout the country and also abroad. The children to whom TEAM played its first show, which was for six- and seven-year-olds, are now nineteen or twenty. Some of them will have seen JACKO, THEN MOSES MET MARCONI, and BORDERLANDS in the past few years. They have grown up with TEAM and that is why this book is dedicated to them.

THEATRE-IN-EDUCATION

Theatre-in-Education began in 1965 in the Belgrade Theatre, Coventry and has developed apace since then. There are dozens of British T.I.E. companies and indeed Wales has one company for each of its six counties. In Britain therefore T.I.E. is rightly referred to as 'a movement'. It is a significant section of the theatre world and a not unimportant educational resource.

The philosophy of T.I.E. arose from the broader debate in the sixties about the relationship between various social services and the community they were established to serve. That decade saw the growth of community and comprehensive schools and the development of adult and continuing education. There was considerable debate about the school curriculum, and about the need to make education more child-centred and experiential. Similarly, in the field of the arts there was the growth of arts centres, community arts schemes, and a general awareness that the arts were a resource for all the community and that artists had a social and political role beyond the production of art for art's sake. Out of those impulses, reflected in the arts and education, arose the desire among some actors to do work for young people in schools and youth clubs. It was then that the pattern of opening theatres to schools and of developing short pieces which were presented on visits to schools, began to take shape. Soon a few actors, and later many, became more interested in this aspect of their work than in their regular acting and so were born the first theatre-in-education *teams* of *actor-teachers* who developed *programmes* for the schools in their area. At first these teams remained attached to their repertory theatres and many still do, but others were formed independently and their sole *raison d'etre* was as T.I.E. companies.

Such gradual specialisation allowed T.I.E. teams work with teachers in the development of programmes which reflected the needs and interests of the children in a particular age-group. Often these programmes were related to the curriculum, particularly in a subject-area like history, but as teams developed they began to do more and more extra-curricular work and so contribute to the personal and social education of the children through programmes which explored what we in TEAM call 'the world outside the classroom'.

THE GROWTH OF TEAM

TEAM's development as a T.I.E. company follows a pattern typical of many arts organisations in Ireland. It began with a few people enthused by an idea, was continued by others whose commitment outweighed their good sense, and its recent progress reflects the determination of the company not to be patronised in exactly the way children are patronised, but instead to produce T.I.E. programmes whose artistic and educational standards are so high as to make the company an indispensable resource. T.I.E. is a mongrel activity, always in danger of falling between the two stools of theatre and education. What TEAM has managed to do is build a plank between the two and it is presently a much respected theatre company and a much coveted educational resource.

It is a matter of regret and frustration for TEAM that the Department of Education has largely ignored the company's work and gives it no financial support whatsoever. Were it not for the Arts Council's grant-aid, supplemented by a number of V.E.C.'s in TEAM's touring area, and the financial assistance of Allied Irish Banks, the ESB and Irish Cement, the company would be unable to service the school community in the counties it does.

1975-1980: 'PLAYING THE FIELD'

The first five years for TEAM were exciting and difficult. The list of productions in that period, to be found below, demonstrates how the company was pioneering by developing its own skills and experience and by 'playing the field' in schools, youth clubs, theatres, community centres, streets and even beaches! Sometimes the programmes were devised by the company, sometimes they were written by an 'outsider', and sometimes the company presented existing T.I.E. programmes from Britain.

That period grew to full fruition when TEAM produced John McArdle's *Jacko*. This was a major piece of work, accomplished not only in the writing but also in the social analysis which underpinned the play. It was entirely appropriate that TEAM should mature with a play which examined the position of the child in society. 1979 was the International Year of the Child, and *Jacko* was commissioned as TEAM's response to that year and its concerns. Eight years later, I suspect that there are few more worthy or durable monuments to the Year of the Child than *Jacko*.

1980-1987: 'CONCENTRATION'

'Playing the field' was extremely important for TEAM at the outset but it meant that the collective energy of the group was being dispersed in all directions. We reviewed this policy in early 1981 and from September of that year changed to a process of 'concentration'. In the first instance we decided that we could no longer tour the whole country and so we withdrew to ten counties: Donegal, Sligo, Leitrim, Roscommon, Longford, Westmeath, Offaly, Cavan, Monaghan and Dublin. Secondly, we committed ourselves to concentrating our service on senior second-level students for the next two years. We decided that in the school years 1981-82 and

1982-83 we would design and tour four different T.I.E. programmes for fifteen- to eighteen-year-olds. Each school would be visited twice a year with a different programme each time and each visit would last for a day. The programme would consist of the performance of a play in the morning, a drama-based workshop in the afternoon, and the provision of notes for teachers to stimulate follow-up work. So successful was this policy that in the 1983-84 school year TEAM founded a primary school service called IMIRT and this worked in primary schools in a similar concentrated manner. It is now policy to try to tour a different programme every school term and so in any school year we do either two primary programmes and one second-level programme or *vice-versa*.

There is now a network of fifty to sixty second-level schools in the ten counties mentioned earlier that have had TEAM visit eight times since 1981. There is consequently a perception of the company as a serious and valuable educational resource, a sense of theatre-in-education as an important service, and an identification and warm relationship with the actor-teachers, many of whom have been constant visitors for the past six years. Amidst a lot of vague theory about the arts in education TEAM is luminously real. When actors play football with the students at 4 o'clock in the afternoon after school, or when they are in a staffroom sharing the teachers' tea and biscuits, there is no such thing as a mystification about the arts. When members of the company arrive in a remote rural school at 9 a.m., unload the van, perform from 10.30 to 12.30, take lunch, run workshops from 1.30 to 3.30, strike the set and load the van, and and all this five days a week for every week of a term, there is none of the glamour of show-business attached, none of the false adulation encouraged by the popular-music industry. Our touchstone in TEAM has been the notion of theatre as a service just like gas, electricity, water, or public transport. We are funded by taxpayers' money and therefore we offer our service to as broad a range of schools in as many places as we can. We have no wish to be mystical and obscure. We simply wish to be understood.

TEAM'S STYLE OF PLAYING

In pursuance of this clarity of contact we carry no lights, hang no tabs, drapes, or curtains and wear no make-up. There is no room for shallow artifice when you have the privilege of playing to a non-theatre audience in their non-theatre space. Even where schools have a conventional stage we do not use it as that would be to invoke an inappropriate tradition and propose a relationship of unearned respect. It is the characters who must be put in touch with the audience and the actors earn respect by the manner in which they succeed in this. Many of TEAM's shows, *Borderlands* for example, are played 'in the round'. Where the arrangement is more formal, as with both *Jacko* and *Moses*, we set up our own portable stage on the floor of the hall. Thus we are *with* our audience on the floor but still visible to them. In *Borderlands* the audience sat in the set of the huge field and surrounded the action. In *Jacko* the actors were present all the time throughout the play which was set against a large backdrop that said simply and clearly: *Jacko – A Play By John McArdle*. Even with a play as formal as *Moses* the actors, as with every TEAM play, are in the hall to greet the audience, show them to their seats and give them a programme. They do not delegate this important first contact with the audience to an usher or tour manager. Of course this direct contact places an added strain on the actors who are already unsupported by lights or elaborate set, but it also ensures an extraordinary quality of concentration and clarity in the performances. It has recently been recognised in Britain that T.I.E. has indirectly given rise to a style of playing noteworthy for its clarity of characterisation, and its strength of contact with the audience. My experience with TEAM's actor-teachers when working with the company bears this out.

THE WRITERS

Because of the philosophy and practice of TEAM and in particular because we want to explore 'the world outside the classroom', it follows that most of our work must be contemporary, and much of it must be written especially for the company. In the past few years particularly, TEAM has developed an exciting policy of close co-operation with Irish playwrights. Indeed the present volume itself is a concrete result of that policy. The short introductions before each of the plays describe the circumstances that gave rise to them.

What is important to note here is how each of the playwrights felt so nourished by the experience of working closely with TEAM that they have already repeated the experience. John McArdle who wrote *Jacko*, later collaborated with the company to devise and then write *Two Houses*, a T.I.E. programme for nine and ten year olds which TEAM toured for twelve weeks to great acclaim and which represented Ireland at the Fourth International Festival of Theatre-in-Education in London in October 1984. Bernard Farrell, author of *Moses*, adapted *Max Und Milli* by Volker Ludwig of GRIPS Theatre, Berlin, for TEAM, and Frank McGuinness who wrote *Borderlands* in 1984 went on to write another major piece for TEAM called *Gatherers* (1985).

No other theatre company in Ireland has commissioned playwrights in the way TEAM has since 1981. No other T.I.E. company in the world has persuaded leading playwrights – writers whose work was produced at the National Theatre for example – to write for them. This fusion of a young and energetic company marked by a strong political motivation and a deliberately popular style, with the power of dramatic language and the richness of image which these major Irish playwrights command, has resulted in plays of extraordinary strength of social purpose and depth of universal feeling.

YOU HAVE OPENED OUR EYES

It is almost impossible to neatly define the nature and purpose of T.I.E. Some time ago TEAM received a letter from a girl in Roscommon who had seen five recent programmes and was now about to leave school. She wrote to thank the company for the contribution TEAM had made to her final years at school. In the course of her letter she declared: *You have opened our eyes and made us see things, of whose existence we were previously unaware.* It is as good a definition of the purpose of T.I.E. as any I know, and better than most.

TEAM'S PROGRAMMES 1975-1987

SUGAR AND SPICE AND RATS AND SNAILS   Autumn 1975
A play about sex-role stereotypes.

WONDER PONDER TIME   Winter 1975
An entertainment produced in collaboration with the Abbey Theatre.

SAME SWEAT/DIFFERENT PAY   Spring 1976
An exploration of the issues behind equal pay for women.

THAT'S MAD!   Autumn 1976
An original script devised by TEAM with the pupils of Basin Lane National School.

OLD KING COLE   Winter 1976
by Ken Campbell of Belgrade T.I.E. Coventry.

ONLY A STORY   Spring/Summer 1977
A touring show for 6-10 year olds.

HANDLE WITH CARE   Autumn 1977
A programme for 16 and 17 year olds, dealing with the choices facing school leavers.

SCHOOL FOR CLOWNS   Winter/Spring 1977
A seasonal entertainment for 7-12 year olds.

THE EMPEROR'S NEW CLOTHES   Spring/Summer 1978
A reworking of the Hans Anderson classic, exploring truth and dishonesty with 5-9 year olds.

POW WOW   Autumn 1978
On the life and culture of the American Indian for 7-8 year olds.

RARE EARTH   Autumn 1978
A programme about the conservation of natural resources.

WINNERS   Winter 1978
Brian Friel's play about the relationship between an adolescent boy and girl.

JACKO by John McArdle   Spring/Summer 1979
A play for adults and 3rd level students about the child-care services in Ireland and Irish attitudes to children generally.

INNER CITY / OUTER SPACE by Jim Sheridan   Autumn 1979
Play co-produced with The Project Arts Centre, Dublin, about urban renewal in the inner city.

SEVENTY PERCENT PROOF by Art O Briain   Spring 1980-Spring 1981
A play exploring the central place that alcohol holds in Irish life, and the personal and social problems caused by alcoholism. Longest running play in Irish theatre history.

SUNFLOWER by TEAM   Summer 1980
A participatory play for 7 to 11 year olds, exploring good and evil through myths.

WIND OF THE WORD by Mary-Elizabeth Burke Kennedy   Summer 1981
A theatrical telling of the old Celtic legend of Labhraí Lionsigh, the King with donkey's ears.

NOT JUST YET by Art O Briain   Autumn 1981
ROUND AND ROUND THE GARDEN by Jim Nolan
Two plays as part of a day-long programme for 15 to 18 years olds on social attitudes

to physical disability and mental illness. Produced for International Year of the Disabled.

PALACH by Charles Marowitz adapted by TEAM   Spring 1982
A programme on control of the truth exercised by education and the media, centred on the death by suicide of Jan Palach, a Czech student protesting against Soviet-bloc repression in his country.

JACKO by John McArdle   Autumn 1982 and Summer 1983
A re-working in theatre-in-education terms of this play about the relationship between a house-father ad a child in care, and an exploration of our attitudes to children.
   This play represented Ireland at the International Festival of Theatre-in-Education in London in 1983.

THEN MOSES MET MARCONI by Bernard Farrell   Spring/Summer 1983
Written in collaboration with TEAM this play examined local and community radio in rural Ireland, as well as attitudes to women at work. Part of a day-long programme for 16-18 year olds.

RUBBISH by Leeds Playhouse T.I.E.   Autumn 1983
A programme for 7 and 8 year olds on waste, re-cycling and the environment.

BORDERLANDS by Frank McGuinness   Spring 1984
A programme on Southern attitudes to Northern Ireland and on the attitudes of young people in the North. For 17-18 year olds in schools in border counties.

TWO HOUSES by John McArdle   *Summer/Autumn 1984*
Written in collaboration with TEAM this play is a history-based piece for 8-10 year olds, exploring pre-famine Ireland; the concept of 'rent' and the complexity of truth.
   Represented Ireland at the Fourth International Festival of Theatre-in-Education in London.

SNAP!   Winter 1984/Spring 1985
A day-long programme devised by TEAM for 17 and 18 year olds on mental health at home, in school, and at work.

ONE, TWO, THREE O'LEARY   Summer 1985
Adapted by Bernard Farrell from the German original 'Max und Milli' by Volker Ludwig. A co-production with GRIPS Theatre, Berlin for 5 to 12 year olds and their parents.

GATHERERS   Autumn 1985
Written by Frank McGuinness in collaboration with TEAM. Set in the Phoenix Park in 1932 during the Eucharistic Congress and in 1979 during the Papal visit. Generations meet and pass, each member telling their story. Their lives give personal shape to the destiny of their country, its beliefs and bigotries, its loves and losses, its fears and hates.

BECAUSE JUST BECAUSE   Spring/Summer 1986
Written by Bernard Farrell in collaboration with TEAM. A primary school production for 8 and 9 year olds which explores prejudice between social groups. Set in the U.S. mid-west of the 1870s where landed settlers compete with cow-herders for the ownership of the prairies.

BLINDFOLD   Autumn 1986/Spring 1987
A programme chosen to mark Amnesty International's 25th anniversary. Written by TEAM's 1986 writer-in-residence, Neil Donnelly, in collaboration with the Company, the subject of human rights is explored at both personal and societal levels.

TOWNS VISITED BY TEAM
WITH 'JACKO', 'MOSES' AND 'BORDERLANDS'

In many cases TEAM visits several schools in the same town. For example the company spends four days in Sligo, two in Monaghan, two in Moate, three in Longford etc. etc.

In some towns e.g. Ballymote the secondary and vocational schools 'combine' pupils for the day of TEAM's visit.

KEY TO MAP

1. Buncrana	16. Carrigallen	31. Moate	46. Clontarf
2. Milford	17. Boyle	32. Kilbeggan	47. Donaghmede
3. Dungloe	18. Castlerea	33. Rochfortbridge	48. Ballymun
4. Letterkenny	19. Roscommon	34. Killucan	49. Drumcondra
5. Glenties	20. Cavan	35. Mullingar	50. The Coombe
6. Raphoe	21. Cootehill	36. Edenderry	51. Castleknock
7. Stranorlar	22. Bailieboro	37. Tullamore	52. Templeogue
8. Ballyshannon	23. Clones	38. Banagher	53. Tallaght
9. Grange	24. Monaghan	39. Birr	54. Clondalkin
10. Manorhamilton	25. Castleblayney	40. Swords	55. Ballsbridge
11. Enniscrone	26. Carrickmacross	41. Malahide	56. Blackrock
12. Tubbercurry	27. Ardee	42. Raheny	57. Monkstown
13. Sligo	28. Longford	43. Kilbarrack	58. Cabinteely
14. Ballymote	29. Ballymahon	44. Fairview	59. Dun Laoghaire
15. Ballinamore	30. Athlone	45. Baldoyle	60. Glenageary

INTRODUCTION TO
JACKO

It is entirely appropriate that this volume should begin with
JACKO. It is the play which represents the bridge between the first
five years of TEAM when the company was creating a working
definition of T.I.E. and the next five when that definition was being
refined and matured into the present understanding. It is no
accident that the play has been given two different productions by
TEAM, the original one in 1979 and the second in 1982. Jim Lynch,
Artistic Director of TEAM at the time was largely responsible for
motivating the entire JACKO project, and his imagination and
perseverance ensured that the play, despite considerable attendant
difficulties, was finally written and produced. With his production
of JACKO, TEAM 'arrived' as a force in Irish theatre. Not only was
it a major piece of writing, given a fine production, but its concerns
mirrored those of the company so that in a very complete way it was
a TEAM play.

For the present volume Jim Lynch kindly wrote the following
background note:

> JACKO originated in a brief newspaper clipping
> concerning the sentencing to life-imprisonment of a
> young man, on charges of the abduction and murder of
> a nine-year-old child from a residential-care centre in
> Dublin. In the year between its origin and presentation,
> I first investigated the background to this event in some
> detail, and was perturbed by the extent to which the
> circumstances surrounding the case had been played
> down, ignored and even distorted. The decision to stage
> a production based upon the incident produced a wide
> range of emotional reactions, with a high degree of
> hostility in some quarters. It was against this backdrop
> that John McArdle and I sat down together over several
> meetings and attempted to imaginatively recreate the
> sequence of events of which the court case was but one
> outcome. It says something for this process, and for

John's accuracy of re-presentation, that we were later accused of having access to confidential files and conversations. Many of those closely involved in the reality of the case confirmed that the script accurately conveys the spirit of the relationship out of which this tragedy emerged. At the same time, in embarking upon the production, we were at no time interested in an 'exposé-documentary'. Rather, the themes and issues raised seemed to us to be wide-ranging and important ones, as they still are today.

Jim Lynch

In 1981 when we decided to concentrate the company's energies on developing new writing and in the first instance for senior-second level students, there was little doubt that we should produce JACKO again. Firstly, it had not been seen because of various legal difficulties to do with the matters Jim Lynch mentions in his note above. Secondly, John McArdle had done some significant re-writing since 1979. And finally, JACKO represented a benchmark in terms of excellence which we wanted to establish for ourselves as a company and for the writers working with us.

Anyone who has seen either production of JACKO will never forget Mairín Mythen's performance as Jacko. It is doubtful whether TEAM would have produced the play again had Mo been unable or unwilling to take part. In a very special way the play belongs to her.

JACKO

A Play by John McArdle
Commissioned by TEAM Theatre Company

CAST

PSYCHIATRIST, about 30 or 40. A Scot
ANDREW, about 30
SISTER DAVID, 40
JACKO, a boy of about 10. Could be played by a small girl
MRS BOYLE, Jacko's mother
AN OFFICIAL
JOE, 30

JACKO was first performed on April 6th, 1979 in the Youth and Community Workshop, Derry. It subsequently was presented in Wexford Arts Centre, the Ivernia Theatre, Cork, the Project Arts Centre, Dublin, and the Lyric Theatre in Belfast. The company for the original production was:

Jacko:	Mairín Mythen
Andrew:	Padraic Mulholland
Psychiatrist:	Philip Tyler
Sister David:	Barbara McNamara
Rose & Mrs Boyle:	Helen Roche
Joe & The Official:	Dave Marsden
Director:	Jim Lynch
Designer:	Consolata Boyle
Original Music:	Peter Sengotta

The re-written version of JACKO, published here, was first performed in Blackrock College, Co. Dublin on September 23rd 1982. The play toured second-level schools in TEAM's touring area for ten weeks and in 1983 represented Ireland at the International Festival of Theatre-in-Education, Newham, London. The company for this production was:

Jacko:	Mairín Mythen
Andrew:	Patrick Sutton
Psychiatrist:	Ronan Smith
Sister David:	Mary Fogarty
Rose & Mrs Boyle:	Linda McDonnell
Joe & The Official:	Colm Quilligan/Philip Hardy
Director:	Martin Drury
Designer:	Martin Drury
Production Manager:	Vincent Dempsey
Managing Director:	Tim O'Neill

**This play is dedicated
to all children in care
and to those who care for them**

Setting: An open setting which can be used to represent various places.

ACT 1

On one side of stage a table strewn with papers. Psychiatrist taking notes. Andrew comes in, sits on a chair. (Pause)

PSYCHI   Ah, there you are Andrew.

ANDREW   Yes. (*Pause. PSYCHI finishes notes*)

PSYCHI   Good. (*Pause*) Well then. (*Pause*) Now, let's see; we'd better get to work as quickly as we can; there's a great deal to be done and the time's getting short. First of all, let's not misinterpret this question, Andrew . . . (*Pause*) . . . Are you quite comfortable there?

ANDREW   Pardon?

PSYCHI   I mean, we can get a softer chair, that sort of thing, if you want to.

ANDREW   No. I'm all right.

PSYCHI   Good. (*Pause*) Now, before the question, let me say that everything seems to be okay; I've tested almost every-ing, at this stage . . . (*Pause*) . . . Well, the question . . . (*Pause*) . . . Suppose I were to say to you that the tests indicate that there was something wrong with you, would you be glad or sorry? (*Pause*)

ANDREW   I don't know. (*Pause*)

PSYCHI   Well, which do you think, Andrew?

ANDREW   I think I'd probably be sorry; nobody wants to think that there's anything wrong with them. (*Pause*)

PSYCHI   Good. (*Pause*) So would I be right in saying that you're trying to prove to me that there's nothing wrong with you?

ANDREW   I don't know what you mean.

PSYCHI   Well, which would you . . .

ANDREW   Well, does it matter what I want? Aren't you going to find out the truth anyway, no matter what . . . (*Pause*) . . . I mean, you can find it out anyway, can't you?

PSYCHI   Oh yes.

ANDREW   I see. (*Pause*)

PSYCHI   Good. Well, let's move on to the incidents which brought you here in the first place.

ANDREW   Yes.

PSYCHI   Good. (*Pause*) Yes. (*Pause*) Right. (*Pause*) Well now, let's take your first meeting with (*looking up notes*) the Principal, a Sister . . .

ANDREW   Sister David.

PSYCHI   Yes. (*Pause*) Oh, first of all, tell me about her.

ANDREW   She was a strong woman. Business-like. She got things done.

PSYCHI   Were you fond of her? (*SR DAVID comes in, sits at table left*).

ANDREW   Yes.

PSYCHI   Are you still fond of her, even after all that has happened?

ANDREW   Yes. She was a good woman. She gave me the job when I couldn't get one. Coming out of the Christian Brothers, there isn't much one can do; if she was wrong in any way about Jacko, well, I've forgiven her.

PSYCHI   Has she forgiven you, do you think?

ANDREW   I don't know; I'm sure she has; she was as good woman.

PSYCHI   Were you fond of her?

ANDREW   Yes. Very fond of her. (*Pause*)

PSYCHI   Mm. Right. Now, tell me about the . . . You were . . . . You just went and asked her for the job?

ANDREW   Yes. She looked at my references, took me for a walk around the grounds, showed me the place and then brought me back to the office and said . . . (*As she speaks he stays where he is and turns towards her*)

SR DAVID   Right Andrew. Well, your references are good, I like the interest you've shown in the work we're doing here, I like your application, your honesty, your willingness to be helpful –

ANDREW   How do you know?

SR DAVID   It's in your handshake, Andrew. I've seen skilled teachers who'd never make good houseparents, well-qualified people; in this job character's what's important and that's what can be divined from a handshake. You'll make a good, indeed a very good, houseparent.

ANDREW   You mean . . .

SR DAVID   Well, I won't be keeping you now; I'm sure you have to settle into the area, get accommodation, and so on.

ANDREW   Yes, Sister.

SR DAVID   You'll be in charge of fifteen children from morning to night except on days off; you'll have to teach them, look after them; be more a parent to them really; you'll find the work very hard but very rewarding. Till Monday morning then. I'm glad you came, Andrew.

ANDREW   Thank you Sister. I've always wanted to do this kind of work and I'm grateful to you. (*Pause. To PSYCHI*) I was surprised it was so easy.

PSYCHI   Yes. Right. Good. (*Pause*) Can we move on to the children. How do you remember them?

ANDREW   I remember their voices.

PSYCHI   Their voices?

ANDREW   Yes. (*Pause*)

PSYCHI   What else?

ANDREW   The noises they made.

PSYCHI   With their voices?

ANDREW   Yes, and the other noises they made, whistling, banging things. You know, children.

PSYCHI   Apart from Jacko, how many of their names can you remember?

ANDREW   Very few.

PSYCHI   How many?

ANDREW   None now.

PSYCHI   None. Are you sure? (*Pause*)

ANDREW   Yes. (*Pause*)

PSYCHI   None at all?

ANDREW   No. (*Pause*)

PSYCHI   You're sure.

ANDREW   Yes. (*Pause*)

PSYCHI   But you're only two months left there. Surely you must remember the children; you saw them every day for almost a year.

ANDREW   Yes. I know. But I don't remember them. I only

	remember the noise.
PSYCHI	Was it unpleasant?
ANDREW	No, very pleasant. It was the most pleasant sound I could imagine.
PSYCHI	And were the children themselves – did you like them?
ANDREW	I loved them. Every one of them.
PSYCHI	Hmm. (*Pause*) Now, if you can't remember the children, let's try and visualise this situation here. (*looking at notes*) You and some other teachers are out in the yard playing with the children.
ANDREW	Yes.
PSYCHI	This would have happened quite often?
ANDREW	Yes.
PSYCHI	Good. Now try and visualise it and describe it to me as you imagine it.
ANDREW	You mean as if it's happening now?
PSYCHI	Yes.
ANDREW	You mean just describe it as if . . .
PSYCHI	Yes.
ANDREW	In one corner, Rose is playing something with the children, the younger ones. (*as he says this ROSE comes on, miming children by the hand etc., bending down to talk to them*)
PSYCHI	What age is Rose?
ANDREW	About twenty, I suppose.
PSYCHI	Describe her.
ANDREW	Her body?
PSYCHI	Yes.
ANDREW	She's average.
PSYCHI	Average what?
ANDREW	Just average.
PSYCHI	I see.
ROSE	(*aloud*) Ring a ring a roses, a pocket full of posies, atishoo, atishoo, we all fall down.
ANDREW	And she falls down and the children fall down.

(*SOUND of children playing begins to fade in, then SOUND of children singing 'Teddy Bears' Picnic'*)

PSYCHI	And Sister David?

ANDREW (*as SR DAVID comes on*) She's marching. She's playing teddy-bears with them. She's very good with them.

PSYCHI I see.

SR DAVID Right left right left right left. Keep the line nice and straight. (*sings*) 'If you go down to the woods today . . .'

PSYCHI And (*Pause*) any other teachers?

ANDREW Joe. He's at the far side, rolling tyres with them. (*JOE comes on, and mimes activity*) (*SOUND of children louder*)

PSYCHI And you?

ANDREW Me?

PSYCHI What might you be doing?

ANDREW I might be playing 'Rats and Rabbits'. (*by now he has to shout over sound of children and voices of Sr David, Rose, Joe, who are continuing their activities, shouting to children, etc. going out on floor to join others*) All right, everybody in line. If I say 'rats', the rats run to that side and see if the rabbits can catch them before they reach the line. If I say 'rabbits', the rabbits run to that side and the rats try to catch them before they reach that line. Everybody ready? Rabbits! No, no, no. Rabbits that side, rats that side. Hands up the rats again. No, you're a rabbit and you're a rabbit. Now hands up all the rabbits. You can't be a rabbit and a rat at the same time or you'll be running after your own tail. Now, ready again.

SR DAVID Left right left right left right. (*she waits for the line to pass, passing comments etc., mixing into the bedlam*)

ANDREW Right everybody, 'Rabbits!' Run quickly – you'll be caught! Ah, some of the rabbits died; they were eaten up by the big gurly rats. Everybody back again.

(*the sound of children is cut*) (*ROSE, SR DAVID and JOE are off*) (*Silence*)

PSYCHI You remember it well.

ANDREW Yes.

PSYCHI And still you can't remember the children?

ANDREW No.

PSYCHI Mmmm. (*Pause*) And what about Jacko? Can you

remember him?

ANDREW   No.

PSYCHI   Even though he meant so much to you. In effect, even though he's ruined you life you can't remember what he looks like?

ANDREW   I can't. (*Pause*)

PSYCHI   All right. Well, let's take that first time you met him. (*looking at notes*) You described that first meeting to me before, didn't you?

ANDREW   No. I didn't.

PSYCHI   Good. (*Pause*) Well, can you do it now?

ANDREW   Yes. (*Pause*) We were all out in the playing area, playing with the children as I described to you. (*SOUND of children again*) (*Andrew is moving into the yard*) I was helping the little ones play something and one of them was running somewhere when Jacko knocked her down and she began to cry. I went over and lifted her and –

(*he goes over and mimes lifting child*) (*SFX now include a child crying*) (*Rose continues her game. At the designated time Joe crosses the stage*). (*now JACKO runs on and stop, looking down at mimed child*)

You're alright. (*going down to lift her*) You're alright.

SR DAVID   (*coming out and ringing bell*) Isteach libh, isteach libh.

ANDREW   (*to Jacko as he holds child*) What did you do that for? You ran straight in front of her.

JACKO   I didn't mean to, sir.

SR DAVID   Isteach libh, everybody, come on quickly. Bedtime. Bedtime.

ANDREW   Well mean it or not, you should be more careful. You could have hurt her badly.

JACKO   I was running sir, and she ran in front of me. If I hadn't have been looking where I was goin' I'd have seen her.

ANDREW   (*to child*) You'll be alright pet. You'll be alright.

SR DAVID   Come on Jacko Boyle; in trouble again.

JACKO   Yes Sister.

ANDREW   (*to child*) If you stop crying I'll jump you up and down, and go (*raising child over his head*) Wumpa, Wumpa, Wumpa . . . (*continues. Voices of other children are weakening*)

JOE Right you bums. Last in we'll make him the Taoiseach, and that's the worst job in the country. Second-last's the Minister for Education. (*as he passes Andrew*) You have to combine Civics with pleasure. (*Andrew laughs*)

ANDREW Wumpa.

JOE Next is the . . . Janey, we'll have a whole Cabinet if you don't hurry up. Come on, come on, come on.

ROSE (*as she goes in door. To Andrew*) They'll have the dormitory torn apart if you're not in it as soon as them.

ANDREW Okay. (*ROSE off*) (*SOUND dies except for child laughing as Andrew jumps her up and down*) Wumpa. Now you're better. And a swing will make you really better. (*circles, swinging, sound of excited scream from child*) Woooooooo!

JACKO I'm sorry sir, about that.

ANDREW What?

JACKO Knockin' down that kid.

ANDREW Oh yes, it was you. (*to child*) Wooooo! (*child laughs*)

JACKO The trouble with me is I always look where I'm going. And if someone runs across from someplace that I'm not goin' they get the deadner. I couldn't help it.

SR DAVID (*coming back on*) Come on Jacko Boyle. You're always last everywhere.

JACKO Yes Sister.

SR DAVID What are you doing there?

JACKO Talking to the new house father, Sister.

SR DAVID He's not your house father. Run along now.

JACKO Yes Sister. Thanks Sister.

ANDREW He seems to be a bag of fun all right.

SR DAVID A bag of fun to someone who doesn't have to deal with him. I'd better hurry or he'll have a spear through every child in his dormitory. He has my head light the same Jacko.

(*SR DAVID goes off. Andrew does not return to the Psychiatrist. Cut remaining sounds of children*)

ANDREW (*to PSYCHI*) That was it. (*Pause*)

PSYCHI So then Jacko – eh – he began coming to you oftener?

ANDREW   Yes.

PSYCHI   You enjoyed him running around after you?

ANDREW   Yes. He was a funny child. I could laugh at him. I didn't encourage him but I liked his company.

PSYCHI   Why did you have to say you didn't encourage him?

ANDREW   He was in Sister David's charge so I didn't have too much to do with him.

PSYCHI   And did Sister David mind him becoming friendly with you?

ANDREW   No. Not then she didn't, not at that stage. At least she said nothing to me about it.

PSYCHI   I see. (*Pause*) Go on about Jacko. (*Pause*)

ANDREW   Well, that's the way I got to know him. He was always under my feet everywhere I went. I used to chase him and he enjoyed that and he had this water-pistol and he'd squirt me with it and I – the kind of thing he'd do – I mean, I was only a week there and one morning I was studying – I was taking special courses in child-care so that I could do my job better. He came – or his head came around the door. (*getting into position*) I was sitting at the table swotting over a book when –

JACKO   Hello.

ANDREW   Jacko Boyle, are you not in your class?

JACKO   No. I was sent out on a message for the teacher.

ANDREW   Well, are you doing it?

JACKO   No. I'm talking to you. I'll do it in a minute.

ANDREW   Well you're finished talking to me now because I'm finished talking to you.

JACKO   Are you? (*Pause*) Do you mean that? You're not coddin'?

ANDREW   No, I'm not coddin'. (*Pause*)

JACKO   All them books must be very hard. We have a whole lot of books; I call them Indians.

ANDREW   Indians?

JACKO   Yeh. They'd kill you. Swish, theong, aaaaaaahhhh. (*falling to floor*)

ANDREW   Are you all right?

JACKO   No. I'm dead. They got me.

ANDREW   What got you?

JACKO   The Indians. Roll me over and see am I dead.

ANDREW   Indeed I will not; I'll roll you to the door in a minute.

JACKO   Ah do. Just this once: I want to show you a trick.

ANDREW   What trick?

JACKO   Roll me over and you'll see. (*Andrew approaches him bending down*)

ANDREW   All right, just this once and then you'll be out that door like a light.

JACKO   Like a light. No, not with your hands. With your boot. You're supposed to roll me over with your boot and say 'The only good Injun's a dead one'.

ANDREW   All right. (*rolling him over*) 'The only good Injun's a . . .'

JACKO   Grrrr. Bow, wow, grrrr. (*imitation of a dog. He's holding Andrew's leg, almost knocking him over*)

ANDREW   Hey, hey.

JACKO   You see – I've changed into a dog when I was on the ground. Grrrr. (*Andrew is attacked again, runs after him to the door*)

ANDREW   If you come back near me again I'll pump you full of lead. (*Andrew immediately to Psychi*) And then I remember another day when Joe and I were watching the All-Ireland final in the TV room. Dublin were playing Kerry, and Joe and I sat down.

(*SFX: O Heithir: "Bail o Dhia oraibh go léir, a Chairde Gael. And it's the last Sunday in September . . ." etc. etc.: recording of the 1975 Final.*)

(*Sound of commentary. After a while, Andrew begins to rise up and down in the chair. Is puzzled. Looks under chair. As he does, he jumps back suddenly as:*)

JACKO   Grrrr! Bow wow. Bow wow. Grrrrrrrr!

ANDREW   (*going down on his knees*) Grrrrrrrr! (*he begins a tremendous dog-fight with Jacko. At the beginning they circle around each other growling, then an occasional sally at each other. Joe goes over and turns up the sound rather angrily. Then the growling from the two of them becomes almost continuous, Andrew sallying at him, rolling round on the floor etc.*)

JOE   Ah cripes . . .

ANDREW (*holding him up*) One dead dog. I'm going outside and I'll hang you to the nearest gatepost and underneath I'll write 'This here's the deadest doggonest nogood dog you ever did see'. (*sound lowers as he closes door behind him. He's just outside when he gets a kick in the face from upside down Jacko.*) You kicknest dead dog. (*sound of Jacko screaming as he tickles him first in his arms, then on the ground. Then suddenly he jerks back*) Oh! (*he has been squirted by a waterpistol*) Here, give me that water-pistol.

JACKO Won't!

ANDREW Will!

JACKO Won't!

ANDREW Will!

JACKO Won't!

ANDREW Give me. (*tries to grab it; is squirted again. Jacko escapes. Andrew follows him around using exaggerated huge cowboy steps. The National Anthem is on the TV*) Give me that thar gun ya rotten no-good, pistol-totin' half-breed with half-Injun half-doggie blood in yah! (*excited cheering, laughing from Jacko*)

JACKO (*poor imitation*) Reckon ah won't ya no-good house-da; ah'll sen' fer Sister David for yah.

ANDREW That there nun's not around the ranch today, yah no-good lyin' coyote.

JACKO Ah plum forgot that. (*Andrew rushes at Jacko and takes the water-pistol*)

ANDREW Now who yah gonna send for, yah greasy goosepimple?

JACKO Well, ah was thinkin' of sendin' for Gawd. (*Andrew bursts out laughing. As he is laughing he is squirted again, and Jacko goes past him*)

ANDREW Yah see this pair of six-guns? Well, ah'm gonna give them a few whorls like this, an' when ah stops a-whorlin' you's gonna be spewed half-way to Donnybrook. (*As he walks around after him, O Heithir tells it's a goal for Kerry.*) (*Andrew rushes at him, grabs him, begins to tickle him. Excited screaming.*)

JACKO Lemme go. AAAhhh. I'll never say anything to you again if you let me go. (*scream*) I'll do anything for you – I'll – aaaaahhhh! I'll sing you a song if you let me go.

ANDREW   I don't like songs.

JACKO   I'll sing you one that you like.

ANDREW   What one, what song, what song?

JACKO   Any one you like.

ANDREW   You don't know any one I like.

JACKO   You'd like 'The Northern Lights of Old Aberdeen'.

ANDREW   Would I?

JACKO   Yes, you would. AAAggghhhh.

ANDREW   Would I? Would I? Would I?

JACKO   Yes, yes, yes.

ANDREW   Right, well, I'll turn you round and put you standing up against the wall and I'll cast a spell on you and as soon as I cast the spell you're going to sing 'The Northern Lights of Old Aberdeen'.

JACKO   Right. I agree.

ANDREW   You can either agree or disagree; when I cast my spell you won't have any choice.

> I'm a magician, greater than all
> I'll make you big and I'll make you small,
> I'll cast my spell and I'll make you sing
> The Northern Lights of Old Aberdeen. (*action*)

JACKO   Hey, that was good.

ANDREW   What was good?

JACKO   It rhymed. Did you make it up?

ANDREW   Wizards don't talk. You're supposed to be singing if the spell worked.

JACKO   Well it mustn't have worked because I'm not going to sing.

(*Andrew makes a charge at him. He runs, laughing. Andrew shouts after him*)

ANDREW   Some day you'll sing for me. (*he stands looking after him, smiling. Joe, disgusted, turns off* TV. *Begins to go out*)

ANDREW   (*looking after Jacko*) I don't know why Sister David thinks him troublesome.

JOE   Who?

ANDREW   That Jacko kid.

JOE   They're all troublesome; they're all bloody troublesome. (*Exit JOE*)

ANDREW   (*shouting after him*) It wasn't they who lost the All Ireland!

          (*Pause*) (*silence: Andrew is somewhat lost. He turns to PSYCHI*)

PSYCHI   Very good Andrew. (*Pause*)

ANDREW   Is it all right if I go on?

PSYCHI   Please do.

ANDREW   Yes. (*Pause*) It went on like that and at the Hallowe'en party – we had a Hallowe'en party for the children; they enjoyed it very much– he wanted to be on my shoulders all the time.

PSYCHI   Were the other children jealous?

ANDREW   No. He wanted to be on my shoulders all the time but I had to give the other children their fair share too, so I didn't let him overdo it.

PSYCHI   And Sister David didn't mind, did she?

ANDREW   Well she couldn't very well carry him on her shoulders.

PSYCHI   (*both smiling*) No. (*Pause*) Right. So . . . eh . . . you . . . eh . . . You said in your statement that there came a time when you felt you wanted to help him, when you . . . I think you said you felt you had to help him.

ANDREW   Yes. There was one evening when he could have gone to the pictures. Joe and Rose had taken a group out and he should have been in it, but he asked me if he could stay with me and help mind the younger ones in the sandpit when they were playing. I thought it odd at the time. (*SFX of playing children in sandpit fades in*) But he seemed quite happy. He sat on the edge of the sandpit watching them, and if any of them strayed, he ran after them and took them back. (*Pause*) But against that, he'd say terrible things; like once he said . . .

JACKO   Hey, Mr Cleary. That one there's goin' to throw sand in the other one's eye. Will I go down and hit him a puck for you?

ANDREW   No Jacko, no. (*Pause*) After that he came down into the sandpit and began to sing. He seemed happy.

JACKO   (*singing*)   The Northern Lights of Old Aberdeen
                    Are home sweet home to me.

> The Northern Lights of Old Aberdeen
> Are where I long to be.
> I've been a wanderer all of my life,
> And many a sight I've seen.
> But God speed the day when I'm on my way
> To my home in Aberdeen.
>
> When I was a lad, a tiny wee lad
> My mother said to me
> Go seek the Northern Lights my lad,
> The finest sight you'll see . . . / . . .
> (*etc., to end*)

ANDREW   You sing nicely, Jacko.

JACKO   Yeh.

ANDREW   Who taught you that?

JACKO   Sister David. I sang it for the visitors on Visitors' Day, and they clapped.

ANDREW   (*to PSYCHI*) There was a little Mongol child beside him. She was about five, and she began to nestle up to him. I was afraid he might hit her and kept him talking.

JACKO   Were you ever in Scotland?

ANDREW   Scotland? Where's Scotland?

JACKO   Where Aberdeen is.

ANDREW   And I suppose Ireland's where Dublin is?

JACKO   Yeh.

ANDREW   Can you sing 'Molly Malone'?

JACKO   No. Sister David never taught me that one. Hey look, she's holding my finger. What'll I do?

ANDREW   Nothing Jacko. Let her.

JACKO   The skin's all rough in her hand. Can she not talk?

ANDREW   Not yet. She's not able to learn.

JACKO   Did she never hear big people talking then?

ANDREW   She did. But she's not able to make out what they're saying. (*to PSYCHI*) He seemed happy. She was smiling up at him and he began to cry. Just tears; no sound. (*Pause*)

PSYCHI   Did he tell you why?

ANDREW   Yes. He said . . .

JACKO   I want to go home. (*Pause*)

ANDREW   All right, Jacko. Don't cry. (*Pause*)

JACKO   I want to be with Mammy and them.

ANDREW   You will some day.

JACKO   No. Mammy said we'd never. (*Pause*)

ANDREW   (*to PSYCHI*) I tried, I think, to get around it some way. I said: 'Now listen here you ole cow-poke, big men don't cry' – something like that. When I had it said, I knew it was a lie, so I said, 'Cry away Jacko'. And then he began to cry more. Just sobbing, as if he was letting it all go. The smaller children were looking at him, but he didn't seem to mind them at all. I put over my hands to him like that, and he just caught them and put them up to his face and cried into them. They were all wet from his tears. His tears were running down my wrist, dripping off onto the sand. He kept crying like that for a good quarter of an hour, and my arms were getting tired. Then I pulled him closer to me and I held his head on my shoulder. (*Pause*)

PSYCHI   Go on.

ANDREW   After a while, he seemed to have cried himself out, and he was able to say:

JACKO   That's what reminded me. Wee Sheila used to pull my hand like that. She wasn't able to talk either.

ANDREW   (*to PSYCHI*) I said it wouldn't be long till he was home again, though I didn't know anything about it. Then he said:

JACKO   No. Mammy said we'd never have enough money to ever be together again. She said it was because there were so many bad people.

ANDREW   There aren't any bad people, Jacko, and some day I promise you you'll be together again.

JACKO   You mean Mammy and Joey and Liam and Sheila and me? (*excited*)

ANDREW   Yes.

JACKO   No. Mammy said she had no money, but I knew it was because she didn't want us when she had the new baby.

ANDREW   What?

JACKO   She had it to play with and that's why she sent us away. She said she hadn't enough money to keep us, but I know that babies cost a hundred pound, and where did she get that?

ANDREW   Some friend might have given her the hundred pounds, Jacko. You'll see; some day you'll all be together again, I'll bet you. (*to PSYCHI*) Then he stopped crying, and he pulled back from me and he smiled and said:

JACKO   Nope! You ole cow-poke; if me ma says nope, me ma says nope.

ANDREW   I must have played with him or something, and after a while he had forgotten about it, but it made me angry that his mother should have told him that. I thought it was bad enough letting him be put into care, but to tell a child of that age that . . . that there was no hope seemed so . . . And what did she want with a new baby if she couldn't . . . (*Pause*) So I made up my mind to go and see her, and tell her . . . and tell her . . .

PSYCHI   You know now of course that that wasn't a very wise thing to do.

ANDREW   I didn't ask myself whether it was wise or not; I just thought that I had to do something. I had to find out more about why he was there, and all that. It seemed the least I could do.

PSYCHI   Did you tell Sister David you were going?

ANDREW   No.

PSYCHI   So who told you where she lived?

ANDREW   Joe or Rose, I don't remember which.

PSYCHI   And why didn't you ask Sister David?

ANDREW   I must have thought she'd be . . . that she wouldn't like it. I might have thought it would have implied that she couldn't look after her own children – I mean, the children in her care.

PSYCHI   Then why didn't you tell her what Jacko had told you, and let her deal with it?

ANDREW   I felt that Jacko had told me about it. Not her.

PSYCHI   I see. (*Pause*) So you went to see Jacko's mother. You were angry?

ANDREW   Not by that time. I wasn't angry any more, but I wanted to talk to her and see if she could bring Jacko back, or if anything could be done. She turned out not to be as I had expected her.

PSYCHI   How?

ANDREW   She seemed intelligent; she asked me in, and talked about St Michael's. She seemed to know quite a bit about schools. Then some time I was thinking about how I was going to begin talking about (*He is moving to chair opposite her*) what Jacko had said, or how I was going to ask her why the children had been taken into care, and I just sat there, thinking. (*Pause*) (*he is sitting*)

M BOYLE   So why did you come?

ANDREW   Hmmm. I like Jacko, and I wanted to come and meet yourself and his father, and see . . . see how we could help Jacko. It's better to know his parents.

M BOYLE   His father's dead.

ANDREW   I'm sorry. (*Pause*) When . . . when did . . . ?

M BOYLE   Four years ago.

ANDREW   What? (*Pause*) Then how have you . . .

M BOYLE   You want to know how? You want to know how babies come. What age are you? (*ironically*)

ANDREW   Twenty-five.

M BOYLE   So then you know where babies come from.

ANDREW   I'm sorry Mrs Boyle. I don't know why you're . . .

M BOYLE   I know. (*Pause*) I don't know why; I don't know what I'm saying. People like you confuse me.

ANDREW   People like me?

M BOYLE   No, I don't mean people like you. But people from St Patrick's and St Michael's and . . . I get all . . . (*gesture*) You want to know who the baby's father is.

ANDREW   No, Mrs Boyle. Please don't think I want to be inquisitive or anything like that. It's just that I like Jacko, and I wanted to meet his parents and get to know you and . . . I thought his father was still alive.

M BOYLE   No.

ANDREW   Then how long are you married again?

M BOYLE   I'm not. (*Pause*) He's just another man. (*silence*) You look as if somebody took the jam off your bread.

ANDREW   No. I'm trying to think about . . .

M BOYLE   I know what you're probably thinking about; you've probably got lots of names for me. There was a time when I wouldn't live with a man, either, without marrying him. But . . . I'm not apologising for Peter. He's a good man.

ANDREW   I'm sure he is, Mrs Boyle.

M BOYLE   And as soon as he came along, I didn't have to keep the children in or . . . I mean, the fellas on the street – they actually beat Jacko and kicked him; coming out of London I wasn't used to it and . . .

ANDREW   It's a nice city, London. I spent a number of years in it.

M BOYLE   Did you? Then you know.

ANDREW   I was in Whitechapel.

M BOYLE   We had a . . . well, it was only a semi-detached, but there was a garden and . . . (*Pause*) This is different.

ANDREW   Yes. (*Pause*) Jacko thinks he was taken into care because of the new baby, Mrs Boyle. I'm sorry, I shouldn't be annoying . . .

M BOYLE   So he was in a way.

ANDREW   What?

M BOYLE   If the baby hadn't come, he wouldn't have been taken in. As soon as we applied for the Children's Allowance, people from the Department started coming and . . . when they start asking me questions I get nervous and I don't know what I'm saying to them. They asked me who the father was and was he supporting me and Peter couldn't support me without a job and how was I to look after five children with nothing? We kept them for three months with people with briefcases calling every day. In the end they took them away. All I wanted was enough food for the children and some little place where we could all be together, that was all. But they couldn't give me that. (*Pause*)

ANDREW   I'll see what I can do; I'll enquire into it. There must be some way.

M BOYLE   You're a good man. (*Pause*) (*M BOYLE goes off*) (*Andrew turns to Psychi*)

PSYCHI   So then you – what did you – did you go to see someone?

ANDREW   No. I did nothing for a while; I wanted to think it out and how I might approach it. I didn't want to do anything rash, not knowing how these kind of things worked and so on. All this time Jacko was coming to me more and more; he got me to help him improve on his football, and to do pieces of his lessons for him, and one day he saw me carving something from a piece of a fallen branch – he wanted me to show him how to do that too. He became good at it. Very good at carving. (*Pause*) When I thought out what I should do I thought it best to go to Sister David. I thought she'd be able to advise me who I should go to. It was at night, I remember, when all was done. She had Brahms playing. She loved Brahms.

(*SR DAVID comes on. SFX of Brahms playing, low*)

SR DAVID   I find it wonderful, just to pull back and relax and fill the room with his beauty. We all need something like that; some little acknowledgement of the needs of the self, after giving ourselves to others all day. That's what Brahms does for me.

ANDREW   It's nice music, Sister.

SR DAVID   Isn't it Andrew! I often think that if I could teach these children to appreciate Brahms, I'd have taught them how to live, because whether we like it or not, we all live in the spirit. We can't give too much to other people. We have to hold back part of ourselves; that part of the spirit which must be our own. What did you want to see me about?

ANDREW   Jacko Boyle, Sister.

SR DAVID   I knew you'd have to come sooner or later; I've seen how he follows you around. I'm sure he distracts you from the children you should be looking after.

ANDREW   No, Sister. I don't mind him at all, but he told me some things about his mother and how he blamed her for his being here.

SR DAVID   Oh, they all do that, Andrew. They all have to blame somebody, it's the only way they can explain it to themselves. I don't think you should worry unduly about that.

ANDREW   Anyway, I was disturbed by what he told me, and I went down to see his mother.

SR DAVID   Oh. How did you find her?

ANDREW   I got her address and asked the way.

SR DAVID   I meant what way was she?

ANDREW   Fine.

SR DAVID   Did you meet Peter?

ANDREW   No, he wasn't there.

SR DAVID   And the baby?

ANDREW   Fine. (*Pause*) I'm glad I went, Sister, because I found out that the only reason Jacko's here and his brothers and sisters are in St Patrick's is that the pension was taken from them.

SR DAVID   That could well be. You find all kinds of reasons.

ANDREW   It all seemed so foolish to me, Sister David. It costs so much money to keep the children in care, far more than it would cost to have them kept at home. I feel that if this were pointed out to whoever is responsible, then they could be taken home again. The children would be happy – everybody would.

SR DAVID   Andrew, you're so uncomplicated.

ANDREW   But something has to be done.

SR DAVID   You're doing plenty for Jacko, Andrew. You're doing more than your share for the children here. Keep doing that; that's something you *can* accomplish.

ANDREW   But this case is so straightforward. It should only be a matter . . .

SR DAVID   These cases are never straightforward. Something appears simple, you think you'll tackle it, you meet another problem and another and another. Normally I don't like to make too much of the children's case histories known to the staff, it tends to distort their judgement, but I'll let you know this much. Peter has a wife and three children of his own living a few streets from where he's living now. How do you feel about that?

ANDREW   I don't know.

SR DAVID   Then stay out of it. There are other aspects of it which will test your convictions more, and if you're not able to say positively that they're right to be living together, how do you think you're going to be able to defend . . . Oh, Andrew! (*Pause*) Maybe it's that hundreds of cases like this have defeated me. So often I've gone to politicians, got pensions or allowances or housing made available, got this or that fixed up, and the children were back here within the week. When that happens, the children are worse off, the parents are worse off, and you don't know what to do. You've raised their hopes, now they look to you, and if you waver . . . Did you tell Jacko you were going to see his mother?

ANDREW   Yes.

SR DAVID   Then he's waiting on you. You can tell him now you can do nothing, and he'll accept it and learn to live with it. I think if you're really fond of him, you'll do that.

ANDREW   Yes, Sister.

SR DAVID   Good. (*Pause*) Now, I'm listening to Brahms. I'll be more than pleased if you stay and listen with me.

ANDREW   No, Sister. I think . . . I have work to do. (*about to move off*) Thank you Sister.

SR DAVID   (*as she goes off*) Oh, if we had the wisdom of Solomon, the patience of Job, the intelligence of . . . Come to think of it, I can't think of anyone in the Bible who was noted for his intelligence. Maybe intelligence isn't as important as some of us think. Good night, Andrew. (*EXIT*)

ANDREW   (*to PSYCHI*) And she just went off into another room, and I let myself out. That was the kind of her – business-like, a little offhand; it was just her way. (*Pause*)

PSYCHI   Why didn't you take her advice?

ANDREW   I couldn't. I was brought up to think that we should do good wherever we could – help those worse off than ourselves. That's what I'd been told all my life.

PSYCHI   And do you still believe that?

ANDREW   Yes.

PSYCHI   Isn't that foolish?

ANDREW   No. (*Pause*)

PSYCHI   Mmmm . . . So – yes – eh – . . . Your statement says you went to the Department of Social Welfare. Who told you to go there?

ANDREW   I found out; Joe knew somebody who told me what to do.

PSYCHI   So you didn't take the point of this Peter man having a family of his own?

ANDREW   Yes, I did. I thought about it and decided. Whatever I did wasn't going to make life any worse for his real wife. It might make it better for Jacko and his family. So I went. (*Pause*) At first he wouldn't talk to me about it. Refused to discuss the case. (*enter THE OFFICIAL with files*) It was confidential, he said, fingering through files, looking up other files, pretending I wasn't there. I wouldn't take no for an answer, and wouldn't leave. I talked and argued with him; then when he was sure I knew as much about the case as he did, and wasn't going to leave, he said:

OFFICIAL   Now, this case as you know is rather complex. She's living with a married man, the man's real wife applied for deserted wives' allowance. We simply couldn't entertain giving desertion allowance to this man's wife and continue giving a widow's pension to the woman he was supporting – it's ludicrous. We're dealing with tax-payers' money here; we have to be sure it's used well.

ANDREW   But it was so little.

OFFICIAL   Ah yes, every case on its own is so little. But we've got to think of the precedents we set. Give it to them and we'd have a thousand similar applications within a week. In any case, it wasn't really in our hands. The law is the law, and states that a person can't be in receipt of Widow's Allowances if she's supported by another man. We don't make the laws, the politicians do. That's what the people put them there for, and if there were enough demand for changes in the legislation I have no doubt such changes would be made. In any case, it's not our function to judge the probity of laws; it's our job to implement them. Do anything else and there's chaos.

ANDREW   But surely there's some way around it?

OFFICIAL   I have no doubt there is. If there is, our social workers are monitoring the case continually, and if any opportunity arises . . .

ANDREW   Monitoring the case? These children are unhappy. They want to go home. Their mother wants to have them, but if they go home they starve. And you say you're monitoring the case.

OFFICIAL   Mr Cleary. I don't think I can discuss the case further; there might be aspects of it which, if I were to divulge to you, might involve a breach of our principles of confidentiality.

ANDREW   Aspects. What aspects?

OFFICIAL   What?

ANDREW   What aspects can you not divulge?

OFFICIAL   That's not for me to say.

ANDREW   For instance.

OFFICIAL   I'm sorry; I won't be drawn on that matter. Suffice it to say our social workers call regularly, she's the subject of frequent and lengthy discussion among them, and they're very concerned about the case. They know only too well the hardship which can come to people as a result of some of their decisions, and . . .

ANDREW   Hardship? It's not hardship; they're starving.

OFFICIAL   Our workers know exactly the amount of –

ANDREW   She doesn't trust your workers; she wouldn't tell them anything. She thinks they're against her.

OFFICIAL   She doesn't have to tell them anything. They've got all the relevant facts.

ANDREW   And statistics I suppose.

OFFICIAL   Mr Cleary, I'm sorry, but I mustn't discuss this matter further. I appreciate your concern and it's good to meet people who are involved in related fields, but there are elements of this case which I could not reveal to you without being in breach of – just accept that we're doing our best and that we can't do any more.

(*The Official's voice drifts down and conducts a conversation at a lower level while Andrew says*)

ANDREW   He continued talking for a while and explaining that there was nothing they could do, they had so much to correlate, so many cases to look after, quick decisions to make. They mightn't always be right; he didn't claim they were right even most of the time, but he was certain that they tried to look at all aspects of a case before making decisions. I must say that after I had talked to him a while, I had to admit that if I were in his position I might have had to make the same decision myself about Jacko. I don't mean that I think he was right, but given his view of it and – anyway I was out on the street before it struck me that he had said something about the children being –

OFFICIAL   (*raising his voice above a mumble*) . . . left on their own there and abandoned. Well, it simply didn't leave us any choice; we couldn't very well leave them there. That's

the reason I say Thank God for places like St Michael's
and the reason I appreciate so much the work you people
are doing. Excellent work. I mean, where could we have
brought them; well, not me personally, but the staff who
found them – I mean, what could one have done? (*official's voice drifts off again*)

ANDREW   Up to that, it had been my impression that the children
had been taken into care; I'd imagined a big scene with
the mother crying, and all that. I didn't know what to
make of it; I thought of going back to the mother, then
of going back to the department official to ask him more
about it but he had already been called away, and
although he said I could call again if there were any new
developments, I didn't feel I could just go back to him
straightaway. On thinking about it, I didn't feel I should
go back to Mrs Boyle either, so I began to seek Jacko out
so that I could get talking to him in quiet moments,
hoping I might be able to get him to talk about how he
had been brought to St Michael's without making myself
obvious about it. (*Pause*) Looking back on it now, I
realise that he probably thought I was doing it just
because I enjoyed his company – and I did – I . . . We had
nice times together but always someone came or
something happened when we were just going to talk
about it. (*Pause*) Then one day I brought him out to the
sea at Dollymount. It was still early in November.
Things were happening fast now – the wind was blowing
and he was singing into it, as if to defy the winds and the
waves.

(*Andrew skidding stones on the sea. Jacko's voice over
SFX of waves*)

JACKO   (*singing*)   I've been a wanderer all of my life,
                And many a sight I've seen,
                But God speed the day
                When I'm on my way
                To my home in Aberdeen.

(*Pause*) (*SFX of sea, seagulls*)

	It's cold enough here now.
ANDREW	Mmmm?
JACKO	Maybe we should go home.
ANDREW	Where's home?
JACKO	It's in Dublin.
ANDREW	And Ireland's where Dublin is. And Scotland's where Aberdeen is.
JACKO	Will you show me the Gileses?
ANDREW	Gileses?
JACKO	The Johnny Gileses – one-twos and flicks, and all that. I saw you at them; you're great!
ANDREW	I'm not great. I might be great in St Michael's but I'm not great. But you're right, Johnny Giles is great.
JACKO	Yeh. He's livin' in Dublin too now; he had to come back to it. Everybody that's big must live in Dublin. (*Pause*) Where's your home?
ANDREW	Where my bed is.
JACKO	What?
ANDREW	And my bed's where Dublin is. (*Pause*)
JACKO	I'd love to see your house where you live.
ANDREW	Some day I'll show it to you. I'll bring you to it and show it to you.
JACKO	You're not coddin'?
ANDREW	No. It's not a house, it's a flat.
JACKO	That's what we had was a flat.
ANDREW	Did you mind leaving it very much?
JACKO	Yeh. (*Pause*)
ANDREW	Was your mother crying when you were leaving?
JACKO	No. She wasn't there. She was away to the shop. Her and Uncle Peter were away at the shop for two days.
ANDREW	Were they? They must have had to buy a lot.
JACKO	Yes. She had to get milk for the baby. There was very little milk in Dublin that time.
ANDREW	Who told you that?
JACKO	Sure there must have been when it took them so long. (*Pause*)
ANDREW	What were you doing – just running around?
JACKO	No, we were locked in. You see, they had to lock the door so that the Big Fellas around wouldn't be able to get in and beat us.

ANDREW   And what did you do?

JACKO   Everything.

ANDREW   But how did you pass the time for two days?

JACKO   We didn't know it was going to be two days at the time. Ma just said she was going for messages and went away. We had a great time for a while. We didn't nearly never get staying in the house without somebody to stop us doin' things. And then for a while we had pillow fights and everything. Jumping over the beds from one to the other and sitting on top of the stove. We found that it wasn't that hot so we could take turns at sitting on it. It was great. And we made . . . yah see, the wee ones got hungry and that, and I wetted meal that ma had to make porridge. I wetted it and put piles of sugar on it and that was great. We were rushing ye see, because we thought that they'd come back any minute and there was great sport because we were afraid we'd be bet for using the sugar. (*Pause*) So that was alright till it went on and on and the lads tried to break in the door a couple of times and we had to keep quiet and let on we weren't there – they did that a few times every day. And anyway it went on, and the wee ones began to cry for Ma; they'd keep whinging and sayin' they wanted her. I hit them a puck a couple of times to shut them up and it was alright for a while because the way it'd happen is I'd hit them a puck and they'd cry more and then after crying they'd stop and I'd get a bit of peace. (*Pause*) So anyway, I kept wettin' the meal till they got tired of it and the sugar was all gone and the meal and water tasted horrid on its own. Then the rowin' and squealin' started; you coulda heard them in Aberdeen. The worst of it was that they were squealing at me to do something. I got a chair and put it up on the table and tried to get out the window but it wouldn't open and anyway if you got outside all you could do was fall away down so there was no use in breaking out. So it went on and on like that and then they all cried till they got tired of it and they went to sleep. I tried not to sleep because I wanted to give out to Ma for leaving me to mind them and them so contrary and troublesome and to tell her about the trouble I had with them but the first thing I knew that happened was I fell offa the stove and bumped myself, and I didn't bother getting up but just went to sleep there where I was lyin'. (*long pause*)

ANDREW   So, did someone come in the morning?

JACKO   Yeh. The Big Lads that used to beat us came and we shouted at them to bust in the door and let us out but they thought it was a trap – Uncle Peter used to set traps like that for them, get them to do something and when they were doing it, go out and give them a hidin'. (*Pause*) So as soon as we said for them to break in the door, they ran away as quick as they could and left us and never came back all day. (*Pause*) The wee ones kept crying nearly all that day and I couldn't do nothing because they wouldn't take the meal for me and they started saying things like that the pot was full and spilling over and smelling, but I couldn't do nothing and it was them that filled it themselves but then they started to run around in it, like, and I had to clean the shit offa their feet and that and try and clean the floor because they'd go up on the bed straight from the floor and make it all yellow and wet. But they'd do it in spite of me and I could do nothing but sit down in the middle of it and cry because I knew it'd be me that'd get the beating for not having the place right when Ma came home and the stove wasn't warm any more and I wanted the clothes from the bed to keep us warm but they were wetting them and mucking them about. The life was frightened out of me because I thought we were going to be left there for the rest of our lives and I was thinkin' what would we eat. It was like a story you'd be told in school about forests or something when the teacher was trying to scare you. So anyway, when the wee ones saw me crying they were more frightened than I was and they were pushing in on me, crying. If it wasn't one of them, it was the other one. Before that, when we saw the night coming, we started to beat on the door and on the floor but people must have thought it was something else or couldn't hear us. Then when it came to night we were afraid to waken them. The wee ones were afraid of the dark the second night because they weren't sleeping and they were crying

| | with the hunger too. So that was anyway the way it was till morning again. (*Pause*) |

ANDREW   So what happened then?

JACKO   There was sometime that morning when we all went to sleep or we must have all been asleep because none of them wakened me and then all of a sudden the door was started to be broken in. We all thought we were in for a hidin' from the lads and they all started to scream and push in on me and get behind me in the corner. I got the shaft of a brush in me hand and said to myself I'd beat them with it, 'cause that's what Uncle Peter used to use on them when he got them. So when the door was broke in the wee ones shoved into the corner and wouldn't look out and squealed and screamed. These policemen broke it in and some women came in after them and other people. I started to whack at them with the stick but they threw their coats on top of me and stopped me whacking. So then they took us all away in a car and took us here and gave us a feed. It was that long since I had a feed that I ate too much and was sick; I vomited all over the carpet; they must have been cleaning it up for a week after me. (*Pause*) That's all. (*Long pause*)

ANDREW   (*arms out*) Jacko, come here. (*he lifts him up and hugs him. While he is doing it, he says to Psychiatrist*): I lifted him and hugged him. (*He is not looking at Psychi., but all the energy going into hugging*) In my arms he was so small, so light. (*the SFX of waves continues over this*)

SR DAVID   (*coming on*) It simply can't go on, Andrew. Today he was beating another child in class, and when the teacher tried to chastise him, he said – do you know what he said? – 'If you touch me, I'll send for Mr Cleary'. What makes him think he's so special?

ANDREW   (*not moving from Jacko*) I don't know.

SR DAVID   You'll have to talk to him and tell him your name is not to be used in this way. You'll have to be firm with him.

ANDREW   Maybe he should be changed into my group, Sister. I think he's only being unruly as a kind of . . . if he were in my group, he wouldn't be.

SR DAVID   Of course he wouldn't. That's why I wouldn't change him. We can't reward that kind of behaviour or we reinforce it. We ask for more of it.

ANDREW   It's not a question of . . .

SR DAVID   You're getting too involved with this boy, Andrew. Your work's going to suffer, everything's going to suffer.

JACKO   (*SFX waves*) Will you show me the Gileses?

ANDREW   I'll tell you what I'll do; I'll not only show you the Gileses, I'll bring you to Dalymount as well and you can see Giles for yourself.

JACKO   You're not coddin'?

ANDREW   No.

JACKO   When will you bring me?

ANDREW   When Ireland plays France.

JACKO   Where's France?

ANDREW   Where Paris is.

JACKO   What's Paris? Is it a big place?

ANDREW   Not that big.

JACKO   Is it as big as Dublin?

ANDREW   If you're in love you go there, Jacko.

JACKO   Are you in love with Miss Rose?

ANDREW   I don't know.

JACKO   I think she's in love with you.

ANDREW   Is she?

JACKO   Yes. So am I. Will you bring me to Dalyer? Really?

ANDREW   Yes.

JACKO   Wheeeee! Yahooooooo! (*Andrew swings him around*)

PSYCHI   Would you say this was the start of these feelings for the boy?

ANDREW   I don't know.

JACKO   (*as he is swung round*) Wheeeeeee! Yahooooo!!! (*he starts to sing*)

>   Johnny Giles, Johnny Giles,
>   We'll support you evermore
>   We'll support you evermore.

(*He continues to sing this and 'teaches' it to Andrew. They exit shouting out the song, united in their defiance of the wind and waves.*)

INTERVAL

ACT II

Scene as before. PSYCHI is in his position as before. SFX of the city and the engine of a car. Andrew is driving. Jacko sitting beside him.

JACKO   It's great. It goes really fast. What is it, a Ferrari?

ANDREW   A Morris Minor.

JACKO   It didn't take us long. We could go out there again.

ANDREW   Yes, we will.

JACKO   Great! (*as he catches the handbrake they jolt*)

ANDREW   That's the handbrake.

JACKO   Sorry. And what's that?

ANDREW   The gear lever.

JACKO   Janey. (*Pause*) They didn't think it was me, sure they didn't. They didn't expect to see me driving up in this Rolls Royce. Did you seek the look of Joey? Did you see the big eyes of him when we stopped; I thought they were going to come out the back of his head. We should have all gone home in this.

ANDREW   Maybe so.

JACKO   Will we sometime?

ANDREW   I don't think so, Jacko. Joey and Liam and Sheila seem happy where they are. And you're happy enough at St Michael's.

JACKO   Yes, I am if . . . if I could be with you most of the time. I like Sister David but she's . . .

ANDREW   She has no car.

JACKO   No. And even if she had, she wouldn't let me on it.

ANDREW   In it.

JACKO   Yeh. Sheila looks different. Her knickers are not so droopy. She's getting big.

ANDREW   Are you not directing me. Which way do I go here?

JACKO   That side.

ANDREW   Right or left?

JACKO   Right.

ANDREW   Left.

JACKO   Left.

ANDREW   And which way now. Quick!

JACKO   The other side. Right.

ANDREW   Right.

JACKO   Right. Drive round a bit till they see me.

ANDREW   No, I won't.

JACKO   You should drive through them and knock them this way and . . . (*shouting out of window*) Hey, Knogger, looka me. Looka me. Come here Knogger.

ANDREW   Don't be shouting or they'll all . . .

JACKO   Come on Knogger.

ANDREW   Hey!

JACKO   Janey, look at them coming running. Looka them. Fly or they'll overtake you. Beat them a race to the front door. We'll beat you a race to the front door Knogger. Come on, faster. Look at The Brusher. Look at the waddle of The Brusher. Hurry, Mr Cleary or . . . (*SFX of shouting children rising*) Janey, we'll be swamped if they . . . vrooooooom vrooooooom!

ANDREW   Out quick now and get the door locked.

JACKO   Janey, them Morris Minors is brillo.

ANDREW   Quick. Out. (*SFX of children fades. Sr David comes on*)

SR DAVID   Oh Andrew, can you not see?

ANDREW   What, Sister?

SR DAVID   This. Can you not see what you are doing? Setting him up above the others. How do the others feel seeing the most unruly boy in the . . .

ANDREW   He's unruly because he . . .

SR DAVID   He's unruly because you encourage him not to accept discipline . . .

ANDREW   That's not . . .

SR DAVID   Whatever you say, Andrew, that's the way it is. And he's the boy the others see ferried around, brought in your car . . . didn't the children who gathered round the car mean anything to you?

ANDREW   Of course they did.

SR DAVID   Then if you spent as much time talking to them as you do to Jacko, you might find they're just as deserving of attention as he is. How many of them have you talked to like that?

ANDREW   Quite a few.

SR DAVID   Quite a . . . Andrew, does it ever dawn on you that a child like Jacko might look on you as a godsend, as someone whom he can manipulate so he can get a better time round here, more attention from the staff at the expense of . . .

ANDREW   That's what . . . . (*JOE comes in doodling with a guitar, sits down strumming*)

SR DAVID   At the expense of the other children. The houseparent's time is the most valuable commodity here. That's what you're being paid for, and it is to be devoted to the children under your care. What were the others doing while you were out at St Patrick's? Who was looking after them? Who was playing with them? They need to be played with. They need to be trained. They have to get a chance. Leave Jacko to me, he's directly in my charge. Of course, what you do in your spare time and which of the children you talk to is, to an extent, your own business, and I don't propose to interfere with that, but while you're on duty, while . . . (*she stops in frustration. She doesn't leave*)

JOE   Ah yes, yes. She . . . (*pause, doodling*) she can be like that.

ANDREW   It all seemed such a big thing; as if I'd upset the whole place. As if one child . . .

JOE   That's the way with Sister David. She thinks in boxes. 'That child's troublesome, that child's withdrawn'. Every child has to fit. (*pause, doodles*) Box thinking, I call it. (*sings*)

> A gentleman was passing by,
> He asked for a drink when he got dry
> At the . . . (*breaks off. Doodles thoughtfully. Practising the chords on guitar*)
> At the well below . . . At the well below . . .
> (*continues practising*)

The passage of time in this section of the play is measured by his improved proficiency on the guitar. (In the 1982 production the song used was 'Cockles and Mussels'/'Molly Malone'.

PSYCHI   Would you think you were, at this point in time, something of an innocent?

ANDREW   No.

PSYCHI   Might it not have been that coming out of this seminary . . .

ANDREW   It wasn't a seminary. It was a Christian Brothers community.

PSYCHI   Yes. Coming out of that maybe . . . It was enclosed, wasn't it?

ANDREW   No, not very. No. We got out to various things, and we could get permission to . . .

PSYCHI   So, from the time you were thirteen till . . .

ANDREW   Thirteen and a half.

PSYCHI   From when you were thirteen and a half till you took this post in St Michael's, you would have been in a place where you wouldn't have had to deal with problems like . . . love . . . or parenthood or . . . You wouldn't have had any dealings with young people.

ANDREW   That's true. Others in the Community would have, but I worked – well, I told you that yesterday.

PSYCHI   Yes. In the kitchen.

ANDREW   Yes.

PSYCHI   So . . . eh . . . do you think that Sister David might have been right that just because you knew his story and not the others . . . or specifically, why did he seem to attract your attention more than the others?

ANDREW   I think he helped me to understand people. In that way he was like a window for me. Even at his age, he'd seen so much of the world that he wasn't like a child but more like someone to talk to more freely than to anybody else. I found it hard enough to talk to Joe, and Sister David was my boss and Rose . . . I took her for a walk one day in the Phoenix Park, and when I had her on her own I wasn't able to talk. We just walked and . . .

ROSE   (*coming on*) The squirrels are high in the trees, Andrew. They go higher when the leaves fall. Look at how they can climb.

ANDREW   Yes. Marvellous.

ROSE   You're worrying about Jacko.

ANDREW   No, I'm not. It's not that.

ROSE   Then why are you quiet? (*pause*) Do you not see the haze over the city?

ANDREW   Yes, I do. It's nice, isn't it.

ROSE   Are you not curious about that man with his umbrella on a nice sunny day like this? You're an idealist, Andrew. You're so busy changing the world, you haven't time to see how beautiful it is. Leave St Michael's behind; there's the two of us here. (*pause*) I might as well be talking to that old man.

PSYCHI   Were you worrying?

ANDREW   No, not worrying, but thinking. I found myself trying to live up to Sister David's advice about not wavering, and yet, if I were to accept that, then I had to disagree with the other things she said. It made me wonder whether to waver might be the right thing to do and then, when I'd think that, I'd see that I was losing all sense of purpose and . . .

SR DAVID   No, Andrew, he can't go to the pictures this evening; he's been a little obstreperous today.

ANDREW   And I began to think was she right or was I right in accepting what she said, or . . .

JOE   Well, if Sister David says 'No', then Sister David says 'No'. That's the way things are done around here. (*begins strumming during:*)

SR DAVID   He took the good toys out of the press where they were being kept for Visitors' Day. If the people who come on that day see the children playing with battered toys, how much will they contribute to the upkeep of the place? That's the way of the world, Andrew.

JOE   (*singing*)   You'll be seven years a-ringing the bell
              At the well below the valley-o.
              Green grow the . . .
        She's a middle-class woman, you see. They're the two great diseases of the modern world; conservatism and middle-classness. 'Flu and pneumonia. We're making obedient little machines going click click click. Click your toes, click your heels, click your tongue. Do what you're told. It wears you down. (*sings*)
              My cup is full to the brim
              If I were to stop I might fall in

At the well below the valley-o
Green grow the lillies-oh
Right among the bushes-oh

ROSE It wears him down, poor man. Goodnight.

BOTH Goodnight.

JOE 'Goodnight to you and God be with
The teller of this tale and myth.' Who wrote that?

ANDREW I don't know. She's . . .

JOE Shakespeare. Marlowe – some anonymous yob with grass growing out of his ears. It'll probably bother me till I go asleep. Tell us, could you take a woman off my hands; I'm stuck with two for tomorrow night.

ANDREW No, I'm otherwise . . .

JOE Ah well, it can't be helped. No, I see what you mean about that Jacko kid; not but I wouldn't sit up half the night worrying about it. Of course it's right to question things; it's never good to just accept things as they are. Ah well, I may put these women in a wheelbarrow and take them out to Ballyfermot and auction them. Eightpence each the fresh women! A leg or a breast sir? Eightpence each the fresh women! . . .

(*SFX: Voices over: 'Eightpence the pears and apples. Eightpence the pears and apples.' Different voices: 'Hats or colours of the Game. Hats and colours of the game.'*)

PSYCHI Even though Sister David advised you against having anything to do with him?

ANDREW Yes. I'd already promised him anyhow. I wasn't going to break a promise to him. I carried him on my shoulders and . . .

JACKO Come on Giles! Come on Giles!

ANDREW He cheered and . . .

JACKO Out to Heighway! Hey Johnny looka Heighway, looka Heighway! Janey, he never saw him, he never saw him.

ANDREW He followed every kick, kicking my chest and pulling my hair.

JACKO Hey mark . . . Who's that?

ANDREW Rocheteau.

JACKO Mark Rocheteau, mark Rocheteau, hit him a dunt!

Come on Ireland. Oh good man. Good man!

PSYCHI   Was he naturally excitable?

ANDREW   No. Hey, hey, you're pulling my hair.

JACKO   Oh good man. Good man. Who done that?

ANDREW   Mark Lawrenson.

JACKO   Don't be telling them to mark Lawrenson; he's for Ireland.

ANDREW   That's his name. Mark's his name.

JACKO   Come on Lawrenson! Come on Ireland! That Lawrenson's like lightning! Hey behind you! Behind you! Rocheteau's coming behind you. He's behind you.

ANDREW   He thought the players could hear him.

JACKO   Ach, ye eejit you, Lawrenson. I told you he was behind you and . . . Who's that? Good man! Who's that?

ANDREW   O'Leary. He did well, didn't he?

JACKO   Come on O'Leary. Janey, the size of him Da. I wouldn't like him to run into the middle of my dinner! Go through!

ANDREW   Take it easy. You're kicking me.

JACKO   Go through!

PSYCHI   Did you enjoy him jumping up and down on your shoulders?

ANDREW   No, but he did.

JACKO   Go through, O'Leary. Mind yourself – Rocheteau's coming.

ANDREW   That's not Rocheteau, that's Platini.

JACKO   Janey, it's hard enough to remember Rocheteau without . . . Oh lovely! Lovely! Hey, do you see Giles? To Giles, to Giles!

ANDREW   Come on Giles.

JACKO   Come on Giles! In! Go in!

ANDREW   Take him on. Pass him!

JACKO   Take him on! You have it, shoot! Whatcha waiting for? Shoot! Shoot!

(SFX indicate goal)

ANDREW   I was thrown every way. Swaying against the barriers and trying to keep balanced with him on my shoulders. He seemed to be oblivious to it all. Just carried away completely . . .

JACKO   Janey, Janey, Janey, I'd die for you Giles!

ANDREW   I hadn't brought my car; we took a bus home and walked along under plane trees. He was still on my shoulders.

JACKO   Ach it was out of this world. Just out of this world. Seein' everything!

ANDREW   Do you think so?

JACKO   I'll never forget it.

ANDREW   A great win.

JACKO   The win's knocking down the leaves.

ANDREW   The wind Jacko.

JACKO   But they'll grow again in the spring, won't they?

ANDREW   But not the same ones.

JACKO   That's after Christmas, isn't it? I'll maybe be home for Christmas. They'll all be asleep in St Michael's now. Why don't we go home to your house, and I could go in with you in the morning.

ANDREW   You'd have to sleep on a couch.

JACKO   I wouldn't mind.

PSYCHI   This time he called you 'Da' or 'Dad' at the match; that was the first time he called you that?

ANDREW   Yes. I thought at the time it was because of the excitement, but he began to call it to me in more tranquil moments.

JACKO   Janey, it's a gorgeous place. Wait till I tell the other ones about this!

ANDREW   No, Jacko, you mustn't tell them; promise me you'll never.

PSYCHI   Why?

ANDREW   Because it'd only make them unhappy; they'd be jealous of him.

JACKO   Ah Da, this is gorgeous, I could stay here for ever.

ANDREW   You'll be warm enough?

JACKO   Mmmm.

SR DAVID   Andrew, do you realise what you've just done?

ANDREW   Yes, I made him happy.

SR DAVID   Can't you see it's a victory for him?

ANDREW   Yes.

SR DAVID   It's going to cause misery.

ANDREW   No, Sister, every child has a right to happiness.

SR DAVID   Yes, and happiness for these children is security, not this wild wilfulness. You leave me no choice, Andrew; I'm tired talking. From now on, you won't see him or have anything to do with him beyond the normal day-to-day . . .

ANDREW   No. (*Pause*) If I reject him now.

SR DAVID   I'm not giving you a choice.

ANDREW   I'd rather resign.

SR DAVID   Then so be it. This silly business is undermining the authority of the teachers, the houseparents, my own authority. I've got to be able to make decisions and see that they're carried out and I'm going to do that Andrew.

ANDREW   Ah. (*sighs*)

SR DAVID   Let me try to persuade you not to let this . . . (*pause*) You can help ease Jacko back to the position we had before – casual acquaintances, chance meetings; it would be nice for him to have you around. But just discourage any special relationship.

ANDREW   That's impossible. He'd feel so . . .

SR DAVID   The alternative is no relationship at all.

JOE   You'll be seven years a-ringing the bell
                        At the well below the valley-o
                        Green grow the lillies-o
                        Right among the bushes-o.

Ah, yes, that's her, tough as nails. You have to have some admiration for the gut of the woman.

SR DAVID   What do you say?

ANDREW   I'll think it over. I'll have to think.

SR DAVID   I hope that you'll stay with us.

JOE   There's one of them 'neath the stable door
                        At the well below the valley-o
                        Green grow the lillies-o
                        Right among the bushes-o

JACKO   The Dubs is playing on Sunday, will you bring me?

ANDREW   I have to work on Sunday, Jacko. I won't be able to go.

PSYCHI   Was that hard on you?

ANDREW   Yes.

JACKO   Why can you not do it some other day?

ANDREW   He kept asking and probing; he couldn't understand it.

SR DAVID   You're doing well Andrew, just keep it up.

JOE   Another one's buried beneath the well
               At the well below the valley-o
               Green grow the lillies-o
               Right among the bushes-o

ANDREW   It can't be right. There must be some other way.

JACKO   What are you all uppity for? Did I do something on you?

ANDREW   No. I'm busy at the moment. When I'm not busy I'll be able to bring you places.

SR DAVID He's finding it hard, Andrew. We all are. He was very difficult in class today. But another few weeks Andrew, and we'll be through the wood.

JOE   You'll be seven weeks a-portering in hell
               At the well below the valley-o
               Green grow the lillies-o
               Right among the bushes-o

JACKO   Ah Da. I must have done something on you. Just tell me what it was.

ANDREW   You didn't do anything Jacko.

JACKO   Then why are we not friends? Tell me, and I'll do what ever I have to do to make us friends.

JOE   I'll be seven years a-ringing the bell
               But the Lord above may save my soul
               From porterin' in hell
               At the well below the valley-o
               Green grow the lillies-o
               Right among the bushes-o

(*Andrew moves around stage and goes to MRS BOYLE who comes on*)

M BOYLE   No. I can't take him back.

ANDREW   But he's unhappy at St Michael's. He went almost hysterical today. He hates it there. He said so.

M BOYLE   Tell that to the people who put him there. Tell it to them. There's no use coming to me.

ANDREW   I'm coming to you because you must take him back.

M BOYLE   I can't.

ANDREW   Why?

M BOYLE   Because I can't let . . . I'd be afraid of it happening again.

ANDREW   Nothing could be worse for him than the . . . She was
           making nothing of him.

M BOYLE   Did you ever see a child beaten?

ANDREW   She wasn't beating him. She was . . .

M BOYLE   Could you beat a child till it roared and screamed for
           mercy and then go on beating?

ANDREW   Hmm, Mrs Boyle . . .

M BOYLE   Mr Cleary, Sister David might be mistreating him, but I
           know what I myself could do with any one of them if I
           had them back; did you ever . . . Can you understand
           that someone could know in here that they could kill
           their own child?

ANDREW   Hmm, (*Pause*) We've all felt anger, Mrs Boyle.

M BOYLE   Anger? If you've had no sleep for three weeks and
           you're walking a baby all night up and down a room, up
           and down a room – a room with five more people, sleep-
           ing or trying to sleep in it, and you try to give the baby the
           bottle but another child cries because he wants it, you
           don't call it anger. You don't call it anger, because there
           isn't a name for it, because the people who make the
           names never lived where we live. Let me tell you how
           Jacko was taken into care.

ANDREW   I know. He told me. He was locked in here for two days.

M BOYLE   Do you know why?

ANDREW   I can only guess.

M BOYLE   You're damn right you can only guess. Let me stop your
           guessing and then you'll know why. I don't want Jacko or
           Joey or any of them back again. For three months we
           tried to keep them all here. We had no more money than
           would feed . . . You couldn't run a greyhound in
           Shelbourne Park on the amount of food we had –
           porridge and soup – the price of bread; the price of milk
           for the baby. She was cross and I had to look after her,
           carry her around in my arms at the same time. Joey saw
           her in my arms and wanted to be carried. He was four at
           the time. Thin but heavy. And he'd scream if I didn't
           carry him. Scream till I did. Peter used to try and play
           with him to make him think of something else. But as
           soon as the baby was in my arms, nobody would do only
           me. I'd lift him and try to carry the two of them. Peter

couldn't stand the sight of the two of them in my arms because he knew I wasn't fit for it, and he'd try and take him back, and he always ended up scolding him so that Joey then would cry when Peter came near him. Then the baby got sore ears. I'm telling you all this because these are things which could all happen again. The baby's had sore ears since, regularly has, and any time I've brought the baby to St Patrick's where Joey is, he's tried to hit her and beat her.

ANDREW But not Jacko. Jacko's the one . . .

M BOYLE Let me finish. Are you so impatient?

ANDREW Sorry.

M BOYLE For a month I got so little sleep that once or twice during the day, I stood out in the sun at the railings out there and almost fell over them. At night, Joey – he was a light sleeper – would waken her if she slept. He'd just get up and hammer her or pull her hair or something – I'd have to get up, soothe her, wait till Joey slept and I wasn't lying again till she was crying for her next feed. You're-making much of Jacko being chastised; well I beat Joey often. Often. I slapped him. He became more . . . more . . . that he didn't like me.

ANDREW Sullen.

M BOYLE Yes. So one night, I was at my wits end. They should all have been in bed, and they were all contrary, and Peter had a row with Joey over the carrying and went outside. He was still outside, and I was trying to give the baby her bottle, but he just wouldn't stop crying for it. I offered him other things, but he kept clawing at me, trying to take the bottle away. I pushed him off, and he fell back against the bed. He hurt himself. I knew he hurt himself against it; he began to scream and hammer me with his little fists. He was only four and he was trying to beat me. Now it seems so simple and so silly, but at the time, all I could think of was stopping him crying. I hit him again to stop him. He screamed louder. The other children were crying; Jacko was shouting at me not to hit him, but I beat him and beat him and beat him. I think the world of every one of them, but I know I could have killed him – I mean I could have beaten him until he was dead. I

could have. Then Peter came in – luckily. I was screaming, hysterical. I can't say I didn't know what I was
doing, but everything seemed to be on top of me. Peter
put his arms around me and the baby and Joey and the
other children huddled in. We hugged them – I hugged
him and Jacko and Joey and them all; I was crying, trying
to realise what I could have done – frightened by it. But
we all calmed down and I remember we were all so
happy that we all slept just where we were – huddled
together. It was the first night's sleep we all had in an
age. (*Pause*) The next day there were brown and black
and blue bruises on Joey. The teacher saw them at school
– you know the way: 'Where did you get these?' – 'Me
Ma beat me' – 'Why?' – 'Because I was crying' – 'Why?'
– 'Because she wouldn't lift me'. He reported it to
somebody else, and they began to arrive in white coats
and dark coats, weeks of talking, weeks of beating your
head against . . . (*Pause*) I was fool enough to think that
I could make them understand; I could easily have told
them that the child was lying, that he had been beaten by
those hooligans at the corner, but I thought that if I could
explain to them what taking away my allowances meant
to me, they might give them back to me and I'd be able
to live in some sort of . . . not decency . . . I hardly even
want that – but something better than this . . . this . . .
(*Pause*) I wanted to make them see that if you put
someone from Rathgar or Foxrock into this room for
one week with four starving, crying children, any one of
them would have been ready to kill – to hit – to, oh . . .
(*Pause*) So I sat down and talked to them as calmly as I
could and said . . . said . . . (*Pause*) I'm saying the same
to you now, and I'd see them saying to themselves 'Ah
she really is different from us', and then as long as they
could think I was a different animal from the one that sat
beside them at The Abbey at four pound a time, or the
Horse Show, they could always say 'I don't understand
those people; they have a different outlook on life, you
couldn't begin to understand them', then they could plot
and plan how they'd manage me and the children and my
husband – well, Peter – and . . . oh I could go on. (*Pause*)

Then one of them came with a summons to appear in court on a charge of child-beating. There was no use in thinking the judge would understand either; he was hardly likely to come from Gardiner Street or Summerhill. So we packed a couple of things and went to England the two of us. There hadn't been a day without three or four social workers calling, so we felt safe in locking the door, so that the children couldn't go out on the street. It was like them not to come the day they were wanted. (*Pause*) Peter went around London looking for a job but couldn't get one. He went out to Cambridge, thumbing lifts, and dug gardens near the University to earn money to take us back here. He couldn't live at all in London; he had to be back. (*Pause*) Surely I could take Jacko back, but they'd be around with the summonses again and . . .

ANDREW   Maybe we could talk to someone to get them quashed. They can do that kind of thing, I believe. Maybe Sister David . . .

M BOYLE   No, it'd start all over again the same thing. I couldn't stand it.

ANDREW   But the next time the baby'd . . . She's bigger now; you might be able to . . .

M BOYLE   No. I'm vomiting in the mornings again.

ANDREW   What?

M BOYLE   I've six months to go till the next.

ANDREW   Mrs Boyle, why? Do you not know . . .

M BOYLE   Why? Why? Will you go down to the Rotunda and the first woman that comes in in a fur coat will you ask her why?

ANDREW   Well even with this baby . . . if . . . if you could bring them all back I'd help you, or I'd do my best to get you back your . . . if you could get rid of this man . . .

M BOYLE   How do you get rid of a man?

ANDREW   Eh . . .

M BOYLE   Do you kill him? Tell him to fuck off? And who says I want to get rid of him and go back to having the children beaten on the street?

ANDREW   He has a wife of his own.

M BOYLE   Ah yes yes. He has a wife of his own and should be got rid of. He should be gassed because all good Catholics have a wife and two children and a house with painted railings. Get out!

ANDREW   I'm sorry, Mrs Boyle. I didn't mean to . . .

M BOYLE   Neither did I. Be good to Jacko, will you? He's . . . he's all . . . those children are all I have . . . Oh Jesus. If he's unhappy, try and do what you can. Tell him . . . Tell him that his mother's a bitch. (*Exits*)

JACKO   If you'd even take me for a walk, Da. Da, I could meet you outside and no one would ever know it; I wouldn't tell.

ANDREW   Stop crying Jacko.

JACKO   I can't: I never had anyone like you until you came along, and now you don't want me. I hate this place. I'm going to run away.

ANDREW   Stop crying Jacko.

JACKO   I won't stop crying. I can't stop crying. Take me back home with you, and I'll stay for good.

ANDREW   No, Jacko.

JACKO   Then I'm going to run away.

ANDREW   Where to? You can't run away.

JACKO   I will. I will. I will.

ANDREW   Alright. Do what you like, but stop crying. Stop crying.

(*Disco music. Joe at disco*)

ANDREW   Joe, I had to see you.

JOE   What? I can't hear you.

ANDREW   It's about Jacko. He came to me tonight.

JOE   What? Jacko? What did he do?

ANDREW   He came to me tonight at my flat. He ran away from St Michael's.

JOE   To your flat? You mean he left St Michael's and came to your flat.

ANDREW   Yes. I had to leave him back. I had to climb through a window with him.

JOE   You'd better leave him back then. Sister David . . .

ANDREW   I did leave him back. But he cried the whole way. He was almost hysterical. Even going through the window he was kicking and screaming and saying he was going to do it again.

JOE	What? He was kicking and screaming?
ANDREW	Yes, and God knows where he'll go next time if he thinks I won't take him.
JOE	You were right. That was the only thing to do.
ANDREW	But I don't know what to do. Nobody knows how near he is to . . . everybody else thinks he's calm. That's the terrible thing, and I'm the only one who knows he's ready to kill himself. But I can't get anyone to listen.
JOE	What? Something about a sister? Sister David?
ANDREW	No. No.
JOE	She doesn't know about it, does she?
ANDREW	No.
JOE	Good job.
ANDREW	What?
JOE	Good job she doesn't know. It'd be more than your job's worth if she did.
ANDREW	Look, could we go outside and talk?
JOE	What?
ANDREW	Can we go outside?
JOE	Yes. In a while. But there's this woman here; I don't want to miss her.
ANDREW	What?
JOE	A woman. (*moulds breasts on himself*) I'll be out later.
ANDREW	I can't wait.
JOE	Then I'll see you in the morning.
ANDREW	It's no good in the morning. I'd want to see him first thing and be able to tell him something in the morning. You don't know what he's going through.
JOE	What did you say? Will the morning do?
ANDREW	No, it won't do. (*goes off. Joe goes off after his woman. High point in music cuts into a scream, high pitched, from Jacko*)
JACKO	Aaaaaaaahhhhhh! (*a terrible scream. Sr David gets up*)
SR DAVID	Jacko Boyle. What are you doing?
JACKO	(*screams*) Aaaaaaahhhh!
SR DAVID	Put down that stick!
JACKO	I won't I'm going to hit them and kick them till they scream and screech and . . .
SR DAVID	Jacko.

JACKO	Aaaaaaaahhhhh!
JACKO	I'll kill you. I'll kill you. The whole lot of ye.
SR DAVID	(*almost hysterical*) Jacko!
JACKO	I'll beat you all. I'll kick you all. Yous'll all be afraid of me. Aaaaaaarrrrrgggghhh.
SR DAVID	Give me that stick. Jacko Boyle, give me that stick!
JACKO	I won't. I hate you Sister David. If you come near me I'll hit you too. I hate you. I hate you.

(*She moves in on him. Taking evasive action as he tries to hit her with a stick. Gets stick off him. Gets him to ground, gets kicked by him a number of times. All during the following:*)

SR DAVID	Give me . . .
JACKO	Stay back from me.
SR DAVID	Give me that . . .
JACKO	I will – I'll hit you.
SR DAVID	Jacko.
JACKO	Aaaaaahhhhh.
SR DAVID	You're not going to . . . you little . . . you . . .
JACKO	Even if you pull it off me I'll kick you and I'll scrab . . . aaahhh!
SR DAVID	(*getting him down*) You just tried the wrong person . . . you . . . I'll . . . stop kicking! I'll . . . if you don't stop kicking I'll . . .
JACKO	Mr Cleary, Mr Cleary . . . Aaaaahhhh . . . she's . . . she's . . . She's pushing my legs into my belly, Mr Cleary.
SR DAVID	Now will you stop kicking. Will you stop kicking?
ANDREW	(*comes running on*) What's going on?
SR DAVID	He's just hysterical. He's completely . . . .
JACKO	Aaaaahhhh. She's hurting me, she's huring me . . . aaahhh. She's squeezing me and pushing me.
ANDREW	Give me him; give me him. Here Jacko. Here. Here. (*he takes him and hugs him*) Jacko. Easy, easy. Jacko. (*Jacko's crying goes on and on. Sr David getting back her breath. Long pause, then:*)
SR DAVID	(*still breathless*) That's the end of it Andrew. That's the end of it. This is what all this business has brought on.
ANDREW	What happened? What's wrong Jacko? Easy.

SR DAVID	Jacko. From now on, you can't speak to . . . even speak to any houseparent, only me. Nobody. Not Mr Hanbury, Miss McLoughlin, Mr Cleary. Nobody. You'll talk only to whatever teachers you have in class, and to me. If you learn to behave yourself, then we may be able to . . . to relax a bit, but for now . . .
ANDREW	Leave him to me. I'll take him away now and settle him and . . .
SR DAVID	You won't; you'll go now Andrew, and leave him to me and . . .
ANDREW	I won't Sister David.
SR DAVID	Get out Andrew, please. Leave this sorry business to me.
ANDREW	It's stupid and silly and . . . mean and . . .
SR DAVID	Andrew, I told you to go.
ANDREW	(*leaving*) You'll be sorry for this Sister David. It's feudal and futile. You'll hear more of it.

(*Long pause. Andrew goes to other area of stage. Sits. Sound of Jacko gradually subsiding*)

SR DAVID	(*quietly*) Now you can all leave. (*pause*) Now get up. (*pause*) Go to the washroom and wash your face; your eyes are all red. (*pause*) (*Jacko starts to leave, still sobbing*). I'll be down to you after a while Jacko, and we can talk about it.
JACKO	Yes Sister.
SR DAVID	We'll see what happened. (*pause*) It won't be long, if you behave yourself, till you're able to see Mr Cleary again. (*pause*)
JACKO	Yes, Sister. (*goes*)

(*Sr David stays for a minute and then goes off*) (*Pause*)

ANDREW	(*Loudly, as Mrs Boyle comes in*) Oh God no. No, Mrs Boyle; I don't want to have him at all.
M BOYLE	Then why do you want to adopt him?
ANDREW	I don't want to; I said it may be the only way out.
M BOYLE	You don't know what you're saying?
ANDREW	Yes I do.

M BOYLE	You expect me to give him to you just like . . .
ANDREW	No. If you want to have him, you know what you have to do; if you don't do it, then he'll have to stay in St Michael's, and that's hell for him now. I'm telling you how things are; I only said that adopting him might be the only way out. He put the idea into my head himself; he said, 'I'll stay with you and you can teach me . . .'
M BOYLE	What do you think I am? Are you like the rest of them who think that children should be taken from the poor for their own good, and that people should do it graciously, and sign them over to be adopted? What's the difference between that, and stopping allowances for their own good, taking them into care for their own good; I'm sick and tired and fed up of people telling me what I should do for the children's own good.
ANDREW	Listen Mrs Boyle; you're not listening.
M BOYLE	And I won't. Get out! Get away – run! Peter – come out here and throw this beggar's get down the stairs!
ANDREW	Mrs Boyle . . .
M BOYLE	Get out!
ANDREW	(*backing away puzzled*) I was only trying to . . . (*he hurries away*) (*to PSYCHI*): She just threw me out; she wasn't going to . . . she said more than that – I can't remember it. She said a dog wouldn't let one of . . . or a bitch . . . or any animal . . . she . . . (*going over to Joe who has come in with two cups of coffee*) seemed to blame me for trying to do my best for the child; it was as if she resented my doing what she wouldn't do herself. I'll never forget it.
JOE	(*handing him coffee*) All right. Calm down. Here. (*long pause. Andrew calms*)
ANDREW	Nobody knows, you see, what Jacko is going through. He's . . . on the outside, he's calm and composed but . . .
JOE	All right Andrew. Take it easy. (*Pause*)
ANDREW	This past three nights he's come to me at the flat; he was supposed to be in bed here, but in the middle of the night he knocked at my door. It's fine saying 'take it easy', but only I was holding him on the way back last night, he would have thrown himself on to the road in front of a car; he actually tried to.

JOE   All right. But he wouldn't have. You were holding, you see. He wouldn't have done it; people are like that; children are like that. I know it's serious and . . .

ANDREW   Serious?

ROSE   (*coming on*) Well, what's new? (*Pause*)

JOE   We're talking about Jacko. It seems he's been going to Andrew here this past few nights; Andrew had a pretty bad time with him, pretending he's going to throw himself under a car, that sort of thing.

ANDREW   He wasn't pretending.

JOE   Maybe not. Cigarette? (*Pause*)

ANDREW   No. He wasn't.

JOE   It's very difficult, you see, to know what to do. Isn't it, Rose?

ROSE   No, it's not difficult. If he's going to see you at night, then the thing to do is to tell Sister David.

ANDREW   No.

ROSE   Well, unless you want it to go on . . .

ANDREW   It can't go on; I'm just . . . I'm on the verge of cracking; even when I've left him back, kicking and screaming, I can't sleep from expecting his knock again, or the news that he's done something to himself.

ROSE   Then tell Sister David.

ANDREW   She'll try harder to keep him down; there's no telling what he'll do if she tries to repress him any more.

ROSE   No she won't.

ANDREW   You haven't seen him; you don't know.

ROSE   Andrew, you can't play Dad to the kid; that's not the way this work is done; it isn't good for anyone.

ANDREW   I'm not playing Dad; I wish to God it was as simple as you say. Suppose he did do something to himself; how could we live . . .

JOE   All right. Let's calm down. (*Pause*) Let's take things calmly. (*long pause*)

ROSE   (*quietly*) I'm sorry Andrew. I shouldn't have said you were playing Dad; it's an unkind way of putting it, but I feel I have a right to put it that way because I know myself exactly how you got into this, and I know how you feel.

ANDREW   No, you don't, Rose.

JOE All right. Don't get hot again. The thing is that what's the cause of the whole thing is systems.

ROSE Not systems. Ourselves.

JOE Of course it's systems; everything has to be fitted to systems. Even from birth.

ROSE Take a walk in the Phoenix Park, Andrew.

JOE Don't be ridiculous, Rose.

ROSE Or a day at the sea, or on a mountain.

JOE Rose.

ROSE Believe me Andrew. I know what I'm talking about. I remember a time when I was just like you; feeling I was going to be the only saviour of the world, hating it and loving it. Oh, I can laugh when I think of it now. (*Pause*) Get out onto the mountains, they're nice at this time of year; the bracken's beginning to turn russet, and it's like . . . almost golden.

ANDREW And what about Jacko, these children? They can't go up the mountains, out to the seaside.

ROSE (*getting up and going off, unperturbed*) Oh Andrew, there's more to life than these walls, these children. You're going to have to learn; maybe all this will teach you. I'll see you. (*she goes off. Pause*)

JOE Let's look at it this way – you're up against a system, right?

ANDREW Hmmm?

JOE Drink your coffee. We'll talk about it later; the bell will soon be going.

ANDREW I don't want the coffee.

SR DAVID (*off, ringing bell*) Isteach libh. Isteach libh.

ANDREW Take back my cup.

JOE Right. (*takes it. Pause*) I'll see you this evening. We'll try and work something out then. Right? (*Pause*) Don't worry in the meantime; we'll think of something. (*he goes off*)

(*Andrew stays; Sr David comes in*)

SR DAVID So he's been going out to you at night, Andrew?

ANDREW Who told you that?

SR DAVID Rose did.

ANDREW   I see. (*Pause*)
SR DAVID   I've thought about it. I have no choice but to send him to St Patrick's. The alternative was to ask you to go but I admire your general work too much.
ANDREW   Yes Sister.
SR DAVID   What do you say, Andrew? (*Pause*)
ANDREW   Nothing, Sister. (*Pause*)
SR DAVID   He'll get a good training there. Permanence. Consistency. He's intelligent and should do well.
ANDREW   Yes. (*Pause*)
SR DAVID   Sometimes decisions like this are hard to make, Andrew. But I know that in six months time, when you've proved the great teacher you can be, we'll both look back on this and see that we learned something from it. (*she goes off*) Keep your chin up Andrew. It's not the end of the world.

(*SFX crows, footsteps in leaves*)

PSYCHI   So you accepted it just as easily as that?
ANDREW   Yes.
PSYCHI   Why?
ANDREW   I don't know. I think I must just have been tired. None of them seemed to understand.
PSYCHI   Understand what? Hmmm.
ANDREW   When I was leaving Sister David, Jacko was outside waiting for me.
JACKO   Is something wrong Da?
ANDREW   No, Jacko.
JACKO   Listen, will you take me somewhere?
ANDREW   Yes.
JACKO   Really? No coddin'?
ANDREW   No coddin'.
JACKO   Where?
ANDREW   Just for a walk in the Phoenix Park; it'll get us away from here.
JACKO   Great! Great (*SFX of footsteps through leaves increases*)
ANDREW   So I took him for a walk.
JACKO   Cover me with the dead leaves.
ANDREW   All right. Lie down. (*SFX rustle of leaves, laughing*)

JACKO	Hey, don't cover my head.
ANDREW	I'll camouflage you.
JACKO	Take me back home with you. And I'll stay with you for good. You could teach me everything, and I'd never have to go back to St Michael's.
ANDREW	Not tonight, but if you don't come to me tonight, tomorrow I'll take you away.
JACKO	What?
ANDREW	You won't have to go back to St Michael's any more.
JACKO	You mean . . . ?
ANDREW	Yes. Jacko. Yes. Yes. Yes.
JACKO	You mean you'd be really me Da?
ANDREW	(*beginning to cry*) Yes Jacko. Really. (*he lifts him and hugs him, still crying*) To hell with Sister David. To hell with everybody.
PSYCHI	Do you think you panicked?
ANDREW	When?
PSYCHI	All this rushing into things.
ANDREW	I didn't rush into things – I decided things quickly.
PSYCHI	Yes, but shouldn't you have taken time to consider more closely what you were doing?
ANDREW	No. (*Pause*)
PSYCHI	Why not?
ANDREW	Because one of the things life had taught me was to take decisions quickly; that terrible depression on the strand, and the feelings of fear and panic between them came from not making decisions, being afraid to make them. I should have known better, because I stayed seven years too long in the Christian Brothers, going to Superiors and others for advice, when I should have been out building a life for myself; they told me to pray about it and wait; and I saw how they prayed for anyone who left, as if he was a sinner, so I hung on that much longer than I should have. I always said I'd never do it again, that I'd decide and, rightly or wrongly, I'd never regret the decision.
PSYCHI	Do you regret it even now?
ANDREW	No. I know that this knowledge of the purpose of life is almost certainly useless to me now, like a flower that bloomed and died.

PSYCHI   I see. (*Pause*) So you . . . eh . . . Jacko then stayed that night in St Michael's and . . . eh . . . what did you do then?

ANDREW   I didn't go in the following morning. I sold my car and got £500 for it, and after lunch I went to Sister David.

SR DAVID   Come in.

ANDREW   Good afternoon, Sister.

SR DAVID   Ah, good man, Andrew. You didn't come in this morning?

ANDREW   No Sister. I'm resigning.

SR DAVID   Oh. (*Pause*) I needn't ask why, I suppose.

ANDREW   I want to move on. Work somewhere else.

SR DAVID   Yes. I needn't tell you how much I regret it.

ANDREW   Thank you, Sister.

SR DAVID   Well, call up before you finally go and say goodbye.

ANDREW   I probably will.

SR DAVID   Till I see you again then.

ANDREW   Yes. Goodbye. (*pause. Sr David leaves*) Jacko came to my flat that evening again. He had a few things with him, and we left immediately.

(*SFX of bus*)*

JACKO   Hey, where are we goin'?

ANDREW   You'll see.

JACKO   Why are we taking the bus, Da? Where's the car?

ANDREW   I sold it.

JACKO   Why?

ANDREW   For the money. I wanted to buy you things.

JACKO   Me? Things like what?

---

*From here to the end of the play the soundtrack is almost expressionistic, i.e. it acts as a sort of backcloth for the action that takes place on the stage. In the 1982 production we created a track that was faithful to the spirit of the author's intentions rather than a slavish recreation of every noise or sound he seemed to require. The track grew from specific sounds like those of bus and plane to a constant 'mix' in the final minutes of a train running interspersed with an eerie hurdy-gurdy to suggest the strange effect of travelling constantly in an increasingly nightmarish atmosphere. The sense of adventure which characterised the early part of the track and indeed the text was gradually replaced by the sense of figures being hunted and desperately seeking refuge. The constant presence of the soundtrack for ten or fifteen minutes was also a marvellous counterpoint for the absolute silence and stillness required for the final moments of the play. (M.D.)

ANDREW   Things like you never had before.

JACKO   Like trains and . . .

ANDREW   Yes, trains. (*to PSYCHI*) And I bought him a train that cost forty pounds, and brought it along with us. He used to play with it in the lounges of hotels, at the airport. He even wanted to take it out on the plane. (*SFX of airplane*) But I wouldn't let him. He contented himself with . . .

JACKO   Janey, looka. Looka the houses, and the size of them. Looka and the cars, and people like spiders. Janey, these planes is brillo. They're billo.

ANDREW   People will hear you.

JACKO   Where are we goin'?

ANDREW   Back to St Michael's; we'll parachute down.

JACKO   And shoot Sister David.

ANDREW   Bang.

JACKO   No, like run up and in the door and run for cover in the corridor and kick the door in and bang, bang, babababababang! Run away again, into your parachute and up again.

ANDREW   Parachutes don't go up.

JACKO   We'll have one that can. Hey, looka the boats. The ships. Janey.

ANDREW   And then the sea. Out over the open sea. Over the clouds.

JACKO   The clouds is . . . the clouds is below us. We must be near Heaven. God could put his hand in the window and whip us with him.

ANDREW   Lie down quick. Here he comes.

JACKO   (*squeal of excitement, then cut to singing*)
                    The Northern Lights of Old Aberdeen
                    Are home sweet home to me . . . *etc.*

ANDREW   (*over the singing*) And London: Madame Tussaud's, shaking hands with the figures. He shook hands with the Pope and the Prime Minister and . . . I'll never forget the excitement and happiness on his face. And J. R. Ewing – he was a fan of his, and shook hands with him. And then in hotels, he'd keep drawing attention to himself, just cheering and repeating to himself 'Daddy! Daddy! Daddy!' (*Pause*) And even, one morning we went to

Mass and Communion; even there he couldn't hide his excitement. (*song ends*)

(*SFX of a priest repeating, 'Body of Christ'. Getting louder.*)

JACKO	(*whispering:*) Hey Da, the priest has a beard.
ANDREW	That's because he's English.
ANDREW	Do all English priests wear beards?
ANDREW	Shhh
JACKO	Looka, he can move his lips without movin' his beard.
ANDREW	Shhh. He's coming.
ANDREW	Janey. He's like Santa Claus.
ANDREW	Shhh.
JACKO	Santa Claus with vestments.
PRIEST	*Body of Christ.*
ANDREW	Amen.
PRIEST	*Body of Christ.*
JACKO	Amen. (*SFX immediately there is sound of fairground*) OOOOOHH!! (*excited*) Uuuuup . . . dooooown . . . . uuuupppp . . . . dooowwwn . . .
ANDREW	He loved the roller-coaster. He kept cheering and complaining.
JACKO	Oh God, I'm getting sick.
ANDREW	Will we get it stopped.
JACKO	No, I'll see how many I can splatter. Aaaaaaaaand swinnnngggg. Aaaaaaaand swinnnnnggggg.
PSYCHI	And you went up on these things with him?
ANDREW	I had to; he was so excited. He wanted to hold onto me.
JACKO	(*SFX changes to roundabout*) Giddy-up.
ANDREW	(*standing beside hobby-horses*) Except things like the hobby-horses. I stood on the ground and waved each time he came round, and he shouted:
JACKO	Hellooo!
ANDREW	Hellooo! He jumped up and down on it, pulling the horse's ears like a cowboy.
JACKO	(*round again*) Hellooo!
ANDREW	Helloo. (*SFX. Music changes suddenly; circus music effects*)
ANDREW	He had never seen a circus before. The colour, the

excitement, the clowns. I had forgotten myself what a circus was like, and bringing a child to it . . . it was . . . even . . . even for me . . . (*SFX drumroll. Gasp. Bang.*) a marvellous . . . And we took trains everywhere. (*SFX train*) I forget all the places – Crewe, Liverpool, we'd just go into a station and take the first train which came along, without even looking where it was going. Leeds, Bradford, Swansea, Cardiff, back to London. (*SFX voices*) Hyde Park was meaningless to him. He wanted to stand all the time beside an old black man who was talking about his dog, but then there were (*SFX: football chant 'Chel-sea, Chel-sea . . .'*) other places. Football matches, then out to swing simply in the park, for free. I enjoyed the quietness, but he made his own noise; non-stop, gabbling describing what he was doing, like a running commentary. (*SFX: train, Jacko saying 'Bararump' repeatedly*) then more trains, more places, Oxford, Cambridge, Buckingham Palace for the Changing of the Guard; before we'd go to bed each night, he'd act out again all the things he had seen and done that day. I don't think I could describe how happy he was. He kept saying it – 'I'm so happy, I'm so happy'. (*SFX: football crowd, 'You'll Never Walk Alone'*) He kept saying things like, 'If Mammy could see me now', or, 'Wait till I tell them when we go back to St Michael's'. (*SFX: sound of street over next bit, and sound of radio: 'Police in the Irish Republic believe that he may have been taken to England. He has blond hair' etc.*) He walked everywhere; he didn't want to be carried on my shoulders. How we managed to walk so much – it made me think how right I was because at St Michael's, I had always argued that the more children enjoyed themselves and their lives, the more independent they became, and here was living proof of it, walking beside me, trudging, trundling on, boundless, boundless energy. Anything he wanted I bought it for him: chocolate, sweets, ice-cream, things to play with. We went to art galleries too. Even there, he couldn't keep quiet . . .

JACKO   Hey, looka the picture of the man with no clothes.
ANDREW   That's a Boticelli.

JACKO Jeepers, some Bot O Celli, what?

ANDREW (*SFX: station*) We saw at least one film a day, sometimes two. 'Butch Cassidy and the Sundance Kid', 'Bugsy Malone', . . . more trains, more stations. (*SFX: radio 'When last seen, he was wearing blue jeans, a brown jumper etc. almost subliminal*) And streets. He saw a new suit in the window which was what he called the colour of the Dubs, and I bought it for him; one night in Leeds, we were looking for a hotel, and we went past a station, and we just went in and took the first train which came. It was going to Glasgow; travelling through the night. We ended up along the Glasgow docks when the sun was coming up. He was tired, but still chattering. (*SFX changes to street*) Looking at the flags on the ships I tried to tell him where the ships were from, but he was only interested in the colours and the designs and the uniforms of the sailors; there was one ship with Indian sailors, dressed in something like saris, and he wanted to stay watching them, but I brought him through the streets of Glasgow.

JACKO Hey, I thought I saw someone like me in the paper there, will we . . . .

ANDREW Come on, you old cowpoke. I was tired the whole day, but he kept up till we went into a public park and he spent a while playing on the swings, and things, and then I sat on a seat in the park and he climbed up on my knee and wrapped himself in my coat, and before I knew what was happening, he was sound asleep. When he wakened up, he looked at me and he began to cry, and he said:

JACKO Oh, I thought it wasn't you.

ANDREW Hmm?

JACKO Was I crying in my sleep?

ANDREW Yes. I think so.

JACKO I dreamed they took me back to St Michael's and I was there without you – that you ran away from me.

ANDREW I'll never do that.

JACKO Promise?

ANDREW Promise.

(*SFX: trains, circus, playground, etc., during following:*)

ANDREW   We headed off late that evening to Loch Lomond. It was
          late when we got there, and it was almost dark, but when
          we were there, he saw a sign for Aberdeen, and he
          couldn't wait to get there. I was tired but he had to get
          there that night, to see the Northern Lights. It was so late
          when we came to Aberdeen that every hotel was booked
          out, and we trudged around all that night again. For
          Jacko everything was so new that he seemed not to mind
          the tiredness, and he slept in my arms in a bus-station.
          We went to a picture the next day and I slept for a few
          minutes there, but that was all. The tiredness began to
          catch up with me. I knew the police were after us, and if
          anybody came towards me or seemed to look at me, I
          became uneasy. Even booking into the hotel; we booked
          in early – I thought the receptionist somehow – she – I
          thought she knew who I was, and Jacko made such a din
          around the foyer that he must have drawn attention to
          us. My money was all gone and I hadn't enough to pay
          for the room, so I didn't want him drawing attention to
          me, but he kept playing with all the things I had bought
          him. In a way that might have been as well, because at
          least it gave the appearance that we were wealthy.

PSYCHI   So when did you realise that the merry-go-round had to
          end?

ANDREW   I don't know. I knew I – well, when I saw that my money
          was nearly all gone, I became worried because I thought
          it would have lasted longer; it just seemed to go – but I
          think it was in the park when he said how worried he was
          about having to go back to St Michael's that I realised I
          couldn't sustain his happiness any longer.

PSYCHI   So?

ANDREW   That was the nicest night we ever had. I sat there and he
          played with his toys, and we talked – sporadically.
          Neither of us felt we had to talk just for the sake of
          talking.

JACKO   Da, when I get big I'll pay you for this.

ANDREW   Yeh.

JACKO   I'll take you on a holiday somewhere when I'm big and
          you're old.

ANDREW   Where to?

JACKO   Somewhere where sailors come from.

ANDREW   India?

JACKO   Okay.

ANDREW   Then he got into his pyjamas and lay on the bed. If we turn off the light would we see the Northern Lights?

ANDREW   If we don't turn it off, you can always think for the rest of your life that they are there.

JACKO   Yeh. (*Pause*)

ANDREW   (*to PSYCHI*) And that was it then. (*Pause*)

PSYCHI   Mmm. (*Pause*) Do you think you tried every other way before you did this? I mean there was this Mrs . . . this Peter man's wife.

ANDREW   Yes. I went to try to see her after Jacko's mother wouldn't let me adopt him. She had got her allowances and had gone down the country and was happy. She didn't want Peter to come back.

PSYCHI   I see. (*Pause*) Do you like the country yourself?

ANDREW   Yes.

PSYCHI   So do I. I've got this cottage in the Highlands, and every weekend I . . .

ANDREW   The Highlands must be lovely at this time.

PSYCHI   Yes. (*Pause*) So . . . eh . . . (*pause*). Well you seem quite . . . eh . . . frank and . . . well, apart from the memory thing I see nothing much . . . (*Pause*) That's probably not as good for you in a way but . . . (*Pause*) Oh yes. Tell me – what was – eh – Did he just take the sleeping tablets. . . just . . . (*Pause*)

ANDREW   Yes. I told him I was giving him one for each day of the week.

PSYCHI   It didn't puzzle him that you were giving him so many?

ANDREW   Well yes. He said . . .

JACKO   Will I sleep long then?

ANDREW   I told him I wanted him to sleep late because the next night I was taking him farther north, and I promised him that we'd stand at the edge of the sea and look to the north, and we'd see the Northern Lights dancing in the sky.

PSYCHI   This made him happy?

JACKO   I'm lucky I met you.

ANDREW   I'm lucky I met you.

JACKO   I'll see you in the morning.
ANDREW   In the morning. (*Pause*) Then he drifted off to sleep.
PSYCHI   Mmm.
ANDREW   I think he snored once.

INTRODUCTION TO
THEN MOSES MET MARCONI

THEN MOSES MET MARCONI was devised during a three-week period in April/May 1982, spent at the Tyrone Guthrie Centre, Annaghmakerrig, Co. Monaghan. Bernard Farrell and the TEAM company of 1981-82 established the scenario and the characters of the play through improvisation and discussion, and Bernard left Annaghmakerrig with countless pages of notes, scraps of dialogue and even short scenes, several cassette tapes of improvisations, and a head full of sounds, images, and not a few arguments.

Between June and December he cajoled these into a pattern and wrote the rehearsal script for the play. In the rehearsal period (December 1982/January 1983) more changes were made and the play was toured as the performance element of TEAM's second-level programme for Spring 1983.

In April 1983, exactly a year after the initial devising period, TEAM received an Arts Council grant to bring the play out on a public tour and it was seen in theatres throughout the country. For that tour several changes were made to scenes with which we were unhappy during the schools tour. In this way the 'final version' which is to be found in this volume was established.

I had little doubt whom I wanted to commission to write a new play for TEAM, when I joined the company in 1981. Bernard Farrell, I knew, was extremely interested in young people and their world and had been doing a lot of readings and workshops under the Arts Council's 'Writers in-Schools' scheme. I had worked closely with him in Sligo when he did a playwriting workshop with one class of seventeen-year-olds, and I was enormously impressed by his commitment to this work and his obvious rapport with that age-group. There was certainly no doubt about Bernard's professional skills as a dramatist, for by 1981 he had had three plays on the Abbey stage and his I DO NOT LIKE THEE DR FELL was arguably the most popular new Irish play for a decade.

It was important for TEAM to have a 'good' experience if the actors were to trust in this notion of collaboration and it was also important that the company be seen to have the self-respect to approach a major Irish playwright. It is probably true to say that Bernard Farrell had more to lose, but he has always been interested in new challenges, and he quickly accepted my invitation to write a play for and with TEAM. We have good reason to be grateful to him for his courage, for not only did he write a 'smashing' (that's a Bernard Farrell word) play in MOSES, but his act of faith in TEAM increased the company's self-image and its perceived image and so allowed us approach other writers in turn. The centrality of new writing to TEAM's artistic policy in the past few years has already been discussed in the introduction to this volume, and Bernard Farrell's role in the realisation of that policy is considerable.

Very little had been agreed before Bernard and TEAM left for Annaghmakerrig. Though we had had a few preliminary meetings, we did not wish to have too much decided in advance lest we pre-empt the process of creating the play 'on the floor' of the large music and rehearsal room in the Centre. The only definite decision in fact was that the central character would be a woman. This decision was made because in the three plays we had done that year, the main characters were men, and from our workshops with students around the country, we were aware of how deeply embedded were the dominant notions of sex-role stereotyping. Given the opportunity to create our own play it seemed important to favourably discriminate for women. It is interesting how this preliminary choice eventually affected the content of the entire play because one whole thrust of MOSES is precisely an exploration of the role of women in contemporary Irish society. This idea is examined through the private lives of Nuala, her widowed mother Alice, and her engaged schoolfriend, Joan. It is also explored in the more public forum of the pirate radio station where Nuala works.

The radio station, Radio Active, was something Bernard had mentioned at an early stage but which we asked him to bury as it was too strong an idea. Instead we went off on a ten-day odyssey exploring various themes, often related to women. I remember in particular two whole days spent improvising around the story of Little Red Riding Hood. After ten days we reviewed our tactics and decided to reflect our concerns through the prism of Bernard's image of the radio station as the 'vehicle' of the play. At the risk of simplification it might be said that Bernard Farrell brought the excitement and comedy of the radio station to TEAM while the actors gave him the private world of the three women. MOSES shows the real fruits of collaboration not just because both the radio and domestic worlds are present, but rather by the dramatic manner in which they interact. Underneath the comedy there is real exploration of the relationship between on the one hand people's private lives and the quality of personal communication their society encourages, and on the other the definition by practice of public communication as evidenced by a medium like radio.

The issue of local and community radio was and indeed still is of particular interest in Ireland because of the continuing debate in the Dail, the press and hopefully in the streets and pubs, about the sort of local radio service we want to see established in our communities.

†The songs mentioned in this text are those used in the original production. They may, of course, be changed to reflect current trends, but it is important to achieve an overall 'mix' appropriate to a rural pirate radio station. One song, i.e. Meat Loaf's 'You Took The Words . . .' was used as the theme song of Wolfman Moses and it is difficult to imagine how it could be substituted. The songs chosen for the original production were intended to reflect the themes and situations of the onstage action, sometimes sympathetically and at other times, ironically. It is the responsibility of producers to acquaint themselves with the laws on copyright pertaining to the use of recorded music.

THEN MOSES MET MARCONI

by Bernard Farrell in collaboration with
TEAM Theatre Company

THEN MOSES MET MARCONI was written by Bernard Farrell from improvisations by TEAM at the Tyrone Guthrie Centre, Annaghmakerrig, Co. Monaghan. TEAM would like to thank the Board of the Centre and especially Bernard and Mary Loughlin who run it, for their warm welcome and for all the facilities they provided during the three-week devising period. The members of TEAM who devised MOSES were: Vincent Dempsey, Martin Drury, Philip Hardy, Peter Holmes, Gina Moxley, Tim O'Neill, Angela Regan, and Patrick Sutton.

The first performance of THEN MOSES MET MARCONI was given in the Ursuline College, Sligo, on January 24th 1983. The play had a nine-week tour of second-level schools in TEAM's touring area. On Monday 11th April it opened at the Project Arts Centre, Dublin at the start of a national tour of theatres, playing also at the Hawk's Well, Sligo; the Belltable Arts Centre, Limerick; and the Everyman Playhouse, Cork.

Nuala Ryan	Mary Fogarty
Joan Moore	Mairin Mythen
Alice Ryan	Joan Walsh
Declan Murray	Philip Hardy
Bobby Bold	Patrick Sutton
Justin Day	Ronan Smith
Voice of Wolfman Moses	Tom Hickey*
Director	Martin Drury
Designer	Bryan O'Donoghue
Decor	Declan Buckley
Costumes	Angela Regan
Production Manager:	Vincent Dempsey
Managing Director	Tim O'Neill

*By kind permission of the Abbey Theatre.

†See note on page 81.

for Gloria

THEN MOSES MET MARCONI

(*As the audience enters, they hear through the speakers the following cuts of Radio Active's D.J.'s speaking and playing music. The station jingle is heard very often. We hear it now. Then:*)

BOBBY   That's the sign you're on 459 – Radio Active, and now a great sound from a good friend of mine, Mr Joe Dolan.

(*Fifteen seconds of Joe Dolan singing 'More and More'. † Then cut to station jingle and:*)

JUSTIN   Hey hey hey, it's me Justin Day, swapping rocking for rolling here on 459 – the well-dressed one – Justin Day, your own Mr Elegant – the Dedicated Follower of Fashion. Thank you Bobby Bold for some fabulous sounds – hey Bobby what's your plans for today?

BOBBY   Just going to line-up some great waxings for tomorrow, Justin – some raves from the grave.

JUSTIN   Hey hey hey, Justin Day knows what Bobby Bold gets from those Vinyl Vaults: say it Bobby . . . .

BOBBY   Sounds that are gone from the Charts . . . .

JUSTIN   But not from our hearts. See you, Bobby. It is exactly ten minutes and twenty seconds past the hour of three here on Radio Active. This is the Kids from 'Fame'.

(*Fifteen seconds of 'Stargazer'. Then cut to:*)

W MOSES   (*Sinister & Echo*) It's midnight. You listening out there? It's midnight, dark night when guys act brave and the gals take fright. It's me. It's Wolfman Moses, in a bed of blood-red roses.

(*Play opening sequence and opening bars of 'You Took Words Right Out Of My Mouth' by Meat Loaf*)

W MOSES   (*More upbeat now*) Yeah, hi, all you wolves and she-wolves: this is your leader of the pack Wolfman Moses, the creature from the dark side of the moon, coming crawling into your cosy little houses from Radio Active. Yeah, look-out, Wolfman Moses is on the prowl tonight (*howls*) Nobody dare sleep when the Wolfman is about. Now, you listen to this . . . .

(*Fifteen seconds of 'Meat Loaf' brought up. Then cut to station jingles and:*)

BOBBY   Yeah, that's the sign you're on 459 – Radio Active and this is Bobby Bold, rocked but not rolled, feeling cold on this wintry day. Heard Wolfman Moses last night – nailed me to my coffin, but you've nothing to fear, here, with Bobby Bold on wonderful Radio Active. And we're movin' on, movin' up, movin' out here with Brendan Shine 'Catch Me If You Can'.

(*Fifteen seconds of 'Catch Me If You Can' by Brendan Shine*)

JUSTIN   Hey hey hey, it's Justin Day, swapping rocking for rolling here on 459. (*plays jingle*) That's it – Radio Active and now, let's pause for the cause. Today, gang, is Wednesday, Feast of St John the Apostle – okay, you guys, don't knock it if you haven't tried it: it's a Justin Day, Feast-Day. And now here's a smashing one for all you Chris De Burgh fans and hey, hey don't miss his Concert in Dublin next week – I'll be there . . . .

(*Fifteen seconds of 'Spanish Train'*)

W MOSES   (*Sinister with Echo*) It's midnight, dark night, when guys act brave and gals take fright. It's me – Wolfman Moses.

(*Opening sequence of 'You Took the Words Right Out of My Mouth'*)

W MOSES   Yeah, now you listen, all you wolves and she-wolves – this is your leader of the pack, Wolfman Moses from the dark side of the moon. (*howls*) On the prowl.

(*Fifteen seconds of 'Meat Loaf' – then station jingle and:*)

JUSTIN   Hey hey hey, it's Justin Day on another beautiful winter day here on Radio Active. And, gang, today is the Feast of St. Vincent the Deacon: okay, you guys, don't knock it if you haven't tried it – it's a Justin Day, Feast-Day. And here's a forty-five with my Seal of Approval – first recorded by Herb Alpert who was born on March 21st 1937, and here a hit for Boystown Gang – 'Can't Take My Eyes Off You'.

(*Fifteen seconds of this record*)

W MOSES   (*A long howl*) That says Wolfman Moses is on the prowl again – and the time is twenty minutes to one in the dark, dark night. (*howl*) And here's a Wolfman Moses, bouquet of blood-red roses Award. Listen to this, all you wolves and she-wolves . . . .

(*Fifteen seconds of music – heavy. Then station jingle*)

BOBBY   Hi, this is Bobby Bold, rocked but not rolled on the big one: Radio Active – the Station that (*softly*) cares about *you*. Justin Day, your own Mr. Elegance, will be here at seven with good sounds, news and views – but now, it's me, Bobby Bold, rocked but not rolled with sounds like . . . yeah, the Beatles!

(*Fifteen seconds of 'Hard Day's Night'. Then hold under*)

JUSTIN   Hi Bobby – mind if I cut in here with some good words?
BOBBY   Oh hi Justin. Justin Day, folks, looking cool and elegant, all in white with a red carnation – my, my you do look elegant, Justin.
JUSTIN   Sure I do, Bobby – it's what I always say: (*softly*) it's the way you *look*, that tells a lot about the way you are.
BOBBY   You've said it Justin – and we're all looking forward to your show at seven.

JUSTIN   Right, Bobby – it'll be all Go-Go, best sounds around and also Words To The Wise from The Radio Active Good Guys.

BOBBY   Man, that sounds fine on 459, Radio Active. Don't miss Justin Day at seven –   it'll take a good man to beat him . . .

TOGETHER   . . . . but it won't take him long!

BOBBY   You've said it, Justin Day . . . and there he goes, folks – and I'm Bobby Bold, rocked but not rolled – and you're still tuned to John, Paul, George and Ringo: the Beatles!

(*Bring up 'Hard Day's Night' to the end*)

SCENE ONE

(*There are basically four playing areas. Upstage, at back, is the studio of Radio Active. Downstage right is Alice Ryan's room. Downstage centre is an open area. Downstage left will be, at times, Joan's house, a telephone box, an office.*

— It is important that the Radio Active set should remain unseen until it is spectacularly revealed in scene nine —

The radio studio is closest to a realistic set with turntables, kettle, boxes of records, posters, record magazines and a feel of general pop tattiness. At its back is a doorway from Justin Day's flat below.

Alice Ryan's room has a coat rack on which hangs her hat and coat. There is a radio, table and chairs also in this room.

Joan leaves her office at DSL, crosses to centre area – in time to see Nuala walking in the direction of DSR area (Alice's room). Joan carries a pile of office envelopes: Nuala carries a suitcase and a portable typewriter. Both girls are 22.)

JOAN   Nuala (*Nuala turns*). Nuala Ryan!

NUALA   Joan, how are you?

JOAN   What are you doing back here?

NUALA   I wouldn't have recognised you . . . looking so business-like.

JOAN   But what are you doing back from Dublin? Have you just arrived or . . . . ?

NUALA   Just off the train – and it was late as usual.

JOAN   Oh, will you stop . . . .

NUALA   (*Indicates Joan's envelopes*). Let me guess: Mr Moriarty's threatening letters?

JOAN   Oh, just a few Probate Documents – have to make sure they're stamped for the half-six post. But tell me: what was wrong with Dublin?

NUALA   Oh nothing wrong with Dublin – more what's wrong with my mother . . . .

JOAN   Oh, she's not . . . . ? I mean I didn't hear that she was . . . was . . . was . . .

NUALA   No, she's not sick — it's just the way she's been since Daddy died. You know.

JOAN   (*stops*). Oh that, yes. (*awkwardly*). Nuala, I was awfully sorry about your Dad – I didn't really get a chance to talk to you up in the grave-ya . . . . I mean the *cemetery*, but there was such a big crowd of mourners . . . of *people* . . . at the . . . at the, you know – the . . . .

NUALA   The funeral.

JOAN   Yes, the funeral.

NUALA   That's alright, Joan, I understand.

JOAN   He was so popular, your Dad – I never saw so many Mass-cards and flowers on anyone's coff . . . on anyone's . . . (*lost*) . . . I mean, I never saw so many Mass-cards and flowers on it.

NUALA   Yes – everyone was really great.

JOAN   And they were all saying that he went so sudden, Nuala. Last time I saw him, he was just bursting with health. Well, well I don't mean he was bur . . . .

NUALA   That was part of his trouble, I think.

JOAN   What was?

NUALA   His bursting with health. Fifteen stone and smoking forty cigarettes a day.

JOAN   Forty cigarettes a day? (*quietly*) God!

NUALA   I used to try and warn him about it, well we all used to, but you know Daddy – sometimes there was just no talking to him.

JOAN   Yes. (*short pause*) Declan is off the cigarettes completely now since we got engaged.

NUALA   Oh, and how is Declan?

JOAN   He's great – he shaved off his moustache after: everyone says he looks much better without it.

NUALA   And are we any closer to the big day?

JOAN   Well, the house is still being built and with Declan in the business, we think it's best if we have it furnished and everything first. (*enthusiastic*). I was looking at this fabulous suite of furniture the other day – all dark-brown leather upholstery with those tip-up foot-rests – and now I'm only waiting for an opportunity to drop the hint to Declan . . . . (*stops*) But listen, what's your news?

NUALA   Ah, nothing.

JOAN   I suppose you're doing the big strong line up there in Dublin – are you?

NUALA   (*casually*) Oh, you heard about that, did you?

JOAN   (*amazed*) No! Are you really? Who is he? What's he like? Tell me quick.

NUALA   Well, it's all in the past – all water under the bridge. I was as broken-hearted as he was . . . .

JOAN   But who *was* he? How long did you know him? What was he like? Come on!

NUALA   (*nonchalant*) Ah, blond fellow . . . an American . . . said he was in a few films . . . .

JOAN   An American . . . ? In films . . . ?

NUALA   Ah yes, I really miss those candle-lit dinners, gazing into his twinkling blue eyes, his golden suntan and his sparkling teeth, and then driving home together in his Convertible.

JOAN   Convertible what . . . .

NUALA   Ah, but it was the sight of his pink pyjamas that really began to put me off . . . .

JOAN   Pink pyjamas. Now, wait a minute. What was this fellow's name?

NUALA   Eh – it was Robert Redford.

JOAN   I knew you were messing. Now be serious. Who was he, Nuala?

NUALA   Alright – he was just an ordinary fellow: small, dark hair,

deep eyes, sallow complexion, could be funny
sometimes . . . .

JOAN He sounds nice, Nuala.

NUALA Yes. His name was Al.

JOAN Al?

NUALA Al Pacino. You haven't met him now, have you?

JOAN Nuala Ryan! I should have known it! Look, I know what
we'll do: I'll post these now and we'll go and have a
coffee and I'll get it out of you about this mysterious
fellow yet . . . .

NUALA (*picks up her case. Seriously*) Oh really, no, Joan – I
can't. With the train late, my mother is probably already
ringing CIE to ask if the driver has stopped-off for a
picnic!

JOAN Well, then sometime tomorrow – will you still be here
tomorrow?

NUALA Oh yes, I'll still be here tomorrow *and* tomorrow – and,
by the sound of things, a lot of tomorrows.

JOAN . . . But you have your job in Dublin – you have your
Journalism degree.

NUALA The degree I have; the job I don't. I'll just have to look
around for one locally.

JOAN Oh. (*inspiration*) Oh, do you know what you should do?
You should listen to Radio Active.

NUALA I should listen to what?

JOAN Radio Active

NUALA That sounds like a Nuclear Station.

JOAN No, it's the new pirate station here – and Justin Day has
a job-spot on it every evening. It's on four-five-nine
meters and it's great.

NUALA 459 – I must remember that. Well, I'd better go now
before my . . . .

JOAN Listen, I'll give you a ring – and maybe you'll come out
with me and Declan some evening. He'd be delighted to
see you: and don't think you'll be in the way or anything,
because you won't.

NUALA Thanks, Joan – we'll do that so.

JOAN Okay, and Radio Active for the job-spot.

NUALA Great. And say hello to Declan for me.

JOAN I will. (*laughs*) And, don't worry, we'll get the truth

about that Dublin fellow out of you yet. 'Bye Nuala.
NUALA 'Bye Joan.

SCENE TWO

(*Radio Active music is heard as Nuala goes to Alice Ryan's room at S.R. As she enters, we fade this music and hear Radio Éireann on Alice's radio. Alice is 51 but looking older*)

ALICE Is that you, Nuala?
NUALA It's me, Mother.
ALICE Oh grand. Come in and let me look at you.
NUALA (*Bogart accent*) Of all the gin joints in all the towns in all the world, I had to walk into yours.
ALICE (*laughs*) Ah, Nuala.
NUALA How are you, Mother?
ALICE Ah, sure I'm grand. I was just going to 'phone CIE to see if the driver stopped off for a picnic somewhere.
NUALA I said to Joan that you'd be doing that.
ALICE Joan?
NUALA (*kisses her. Explains*) Joan-engaged-to-Declan, Joan. Right?
ALICE Oh Joan Moore, yes. Did you get anything to eat at all. You look famished.
NUALA Now it's alright, Mother. I'll get something . . . .
ALICE Ah now, you've had a long journey.   I'll take that coat
. . . .
NUALA (*Bogart accent*) No-one takes my coat, Blue-eyes.
ALICE Nuala, I wish you'd stop imitating that Humpy Bogart fella.
NUALA Mother, it's Humphrey.
ALICE Well, whatever it is. Give me your coat . . . .
NUALA She was asking for you.
ALICE Who?
NUALA Joan.
ALICE Ah, Joan is a lovely girl. She got a grand lad in that Declan Murray. Do you know they've been going out together since school.

NUALA   Do I know it? Didn't I witness the whole thing.

ALICE   They'll be very happy.

NUALA   (*new level*) Did you go to the choir on Sunday, Mother?

ALICE   The choir?

NUALA   You know, the choir: that gang of Pavarottis up in the organ loft, howling into their hymn-books, cracking all the stained-glass windows . . . .

ALICE   Oh, you were always too smart, Nuala – your sister always said that.

NUALA   Oh, Carol said that I was too smart?

ALICE   She did – and she was right.

NUALA   But Mother, she's the one who is out in California sitting in the sun, with a coke and a smile. I think that makes her pretty smart.

ALICE   Ah now, Carol did very well, Nuala – married a grand chap.

NUALA   Well, we all can't have everything in life. Now, did you?

ALICE   (*teasing*) Did I have everything in life?

NUALA   Did you go to the choir on Sunday?

ALICE   (*testily*) Ah Nuala, how could I go to the choir and your father only dead five weeks.

NUALA   (*seriously*) Mother, you'll have to get out sometime – you can't spend the rest of your life in here listening to the radio and playing Patience and waiting for telephone calls.

ALICE   I like playing Patience.

NUALA   But you're only fifty-one Mother, you've half your life ahead of you. What *are* you listening to anyway?

ALICE   Ah, I don't know why I put it on. It's the Farm Diary programme that your father used to listen to . . . .

NUALA   (*brightly*) Now, Joan – Joan-engaged-to-Declan, Joan – was telling me about a new Station called Radio Active. We'll see if we can find it. It's a Pirate Radio Station.

ALICE   Pirate? Are you asking me to listen to a pirate?

(*Tunes to Radio Active. ABBA is playing*)

NUALA   There it is!

ALICE   (*concerned*) Nuala, you needn't be worrying about me . . .

NUALA   (*laughs*) I'm not worrying about you Mother – I'm worrying about me. I'll have to get a job in this town. Joan says there's a Justin Day on this Station and he talks about jobs and that sort of thing . . . .

(*We suddenly hear the song end on Radio Active, then:*)

JUSTIN   And now from me Justin Day, a pause for the cause: today, gang, is January twenty-first, the Feast of St Agnes, Virgin and Martyr – okay you guys, don't knock it if you haven't tried it – it's a Justin Day Feast-Day. The time is precisely six twenty-seven and thirty-five seconds. Let's boogie down . . . .

(*Music is heard: then we cut to:*)

ALICE   Well now, isn't that nice. St Agnes and all there now . . . .

NUALA   And the time as well – to the nearest split-second.

ALICE   But I have a grand clock that your father and I . . .

NUALA   Mother, I'm not asking you to listen out for the time – I'm asking you to listen out for the mention of a job, anywhere, doing anything. And if they mention two jobs – we'll go as a team! (*Bogart voice*) But if they mention three, well we'll just have to rub one out, blue-eyes.

ALICE   Nuala, what on earth are you talking about?

NUALA   Alright, let's change the subject. Let's talk about food.

ALICE   That's more like it. I'll have something ready for you in a minute.

(*Radio Active jingle is heard. Then we cut to:*)

BOBBY   Radio Active, where the time is eight-thirty, and this is Bobby Bold, rocked but not rolled and these are The Boomtown Rats.

(*We hear the opening of 'I Don't Like Mondays' and fade*)

SCENE THREE

(*Declan and Joan bound into DSC area – a street. Very physical horse-play at first. Declan – 25 and assured – carries a billiard cue*)

JOAN Declan, you can't walk around the town holding it like that!

DECLAN (*aims*) But you don't know what it is. It could be a rifle – and this is how you hold a rifle.

JOAN It isn't a rifle – it's a billiard cue.

DECLAN Clever girl. Here, will you hold it a minute (*gives Joan the cue*) I've got something I want to show you.

JOAN Show me? What is it?

DECLAN (*searches his pockets*) I told you – it's a surprise. (*sees how she holds the cue*) Ah Joan – don't swing it like that – that's my championship cue.

JOAN (*sing-song*) Sor-ry. (*pause as she watches him searching*) Was I telling you I met Nuala Ryan?

DECLAN (*searching*) What? Oh yeah, you told me on the 'phone. Did she mention the Mass-card we sent her?

JOAN I think she did – but she apologised for not giving us an engagement present.

DECLAN Well, I wouldn't have expected that after her father dropping dead.

JOAN That's what I told her – I said we didn't expect it. (*Declan finds the envelope*) And she just looked at me – and, God, I felt so sorry for her, Declan: coming back from Dublin without a job and her father after dropping . . . and her father dying so suddenly.

DECLAN Yeah, rough alright. (*the surprise*) Joan, guess . . . .

JOAN Declan, how many cigarettes did you smoke before you gave them up?

DECLAN What? Oh, about forty-a-day. Why?

JOAN Did you? God! You're not going back on them, are you?

DECLAN Going back? No, why would I? Look, guess what . . . .

JOAN (*thoughtfully*) She said that she has to look for a job now – I told her about the Justin Day job-spot on Radio Active.

DECLAN Joannie, do you want to know about this surprise or not?

JOAN Sorry love – of course I do. What have you got there?

DECLAN   (*teasing*) You wouldn't prefer to go on talking about funerals or cigarettes or Nuala Ryan?

JOAN   (*laughing*) I've forgotten all about them. What's your news?

DECLAN   Right – wait for it: (*shows the envelope*) the House Deeds are signed – and here's the letter to prove it!

JOAN   No! Really?

DECLAN   With a quick flick of the pen, my name went on the dotted line.

JOAN   Which means?

DECLAN   Which means – that the house is ours!

JOAN   (*jumps excitedly into his arms*) Declan, why didn't you tell me on the 'phone? (*kisses him*)

DECLAN   Joan, mind my cue! (*tenderly*) I didn't tell you on the 'phone because I wanted us to be close to a watering-hole for a little celebration. Like the Crescent Lounge over there.

JOAN   Come on then – I'll buy you a big creamy pint.

DECLAN   You certainly will not – I buy the drinks around here.

JOAN   No – I insist. Mr Moriarity is going to give me a rise: he says it's an engagement present for his perfect secretary.

DECLAN   A rise? From a solicitor?? This calls for a few drinks!

JOAN   And Declan – why don't we ring Nuala and ask her to come down and join us.

DECLAN   (*laughs*) Join us? Why, are we coming apart?!

JOAN   No seriously, Declan – she's sitting at home with that mother of hers, scouring the papers for a job . . . we could 'phone her this evening and if she's sitting in, maybe ask her . . . .

DECLAN   Yeah, okay love. That's one of the corporal works of mercy, isn't it: visiting the naked, burying the hungry, feeding the dead and bringing Nuala Ryan for a drink . . . .

JOAN   (*hugs him*) You're a right devil, Declan Murray – but I still love you.

(*Bring in hard the spoken line 'I bet you say that to all the guys' from the Meatloaf record, and let it run into Wolfman Moses music for the bridge into the next scene.*)

SCENE FOUR

(*Now, in the DSR area, Joan is combing her hair and polishing her nails – getting ready for going out – and listening to:*)

W MOSES   It's dark, children. It's ten o'clock, and this is Wolfman Moses here on Radio Active and the Wolfman knows that all you wolves and she-wolves are busy combing your hair and polishing your fangs to go out on the prowl tonight. And the Wolfman Moses will arise from his bed of blood-red roses and will be . . . prowling and howling in the night (*howl*) . . . so watch out and be careful and listen to this now . . . .

(*Fifteen seconds of 'Chantilly Lace' by the Big Bopper and fade. During this Joan goes to her 'phone and dials out.*)

(*Lights up now on Alice Ryan's room. The 'phone rings.*)

ALICE   (*answering 'phone*) Mrs Alice Ryan speaking.

JOAN   Oh hello, Mrs Ryan. This is Joan Moore.

ALICE   Ah hello Joan – nice to hear from you, and how are your parents?

JOAN   They're grand, Mrs Ryan: still going to the Bridge morning, noon and night.

ALICE   Are they? And Declan – how is your Declan?

JOAN   Oh he's great. We're going up to Dublin on the 27th for the Chris De Burgh Concert. It's part of Declan's birthday present for me.

ALICE   Oh now, isn't that nice.

JOAN   Oh . . . oh and you're keeping well, are you?

ALICE   Ah . . . a bit lonely for Joe, but sure what can we do.

JOAN   Yes.

ALICE   Did you want to speak to Nuala, Joan?

JOAN   Yes, if she's there I'd like to have a word with her.

ALICE   Hold on now, love. (*to Nuala*) It's Joan Moore for you.

NUALA   (*to Alice*) Thanks. (*into 'phone*) Don't tell me: you're pregnant!

ALICE   (*quietly*) Oh merciful God!

JOAN   (*laughs*) Oh, that's what goes on up in Dublin, is it? No

	– remember we almost arranged that drink? Well, Declan is calling over for me in the car soon, we can pick you up and go to the Crescent. We're going to celebrate tonight – Declan signed the Deeds for the house today.
NUALA	Oh that's great, Joan, but listen I don't think I can . . . .
JOAN	For a quick one? Come on, sure you might as well . . . .
NUALA	Well . . . there's a lot of things I have to do . . . .
ALICE	(*whispers*) Go on, Nuala. I'll be alright.
JOAN	I'll tell you what we could do then . . . (*Declan enters*) Ah, here comes Declan now – he'll be delighted to see you. (*jokes to Declan*) Remember he had that big crush on your sister Carol before she went to California.
DECLAN	(*shouts into 'phone*) Rumours. All rumours.
NUALA	(*weakly*) Hello Declan . . . .
JOAN	(*to Declan*) That's what you say!
DECLAN	(*into 'phone*) Don't mind her, Nuala. (*cuddles Joan*)
JOAN	(*giggles wildly*) Stop it, Declan, stop it. (*pause, more composed into 'phone*) Sorry about that Nuala – he's a fierce messer, that fella. Will you say you'll come, sure you might as well . . . .
NUALA	I'd love to, Joan – but not tonight . . . .
JOAN	Oh Nuala . . . for just half an hour.
ALICE	(*whispers*) I can be listening here to the radio . . . .
NUALA	(*into 'phone*) Maybe next week – if you're going . . . .
JOAN	(*sadly*) Oh, Nuala. Okay. Next week, then?
NUALA	Great, Joan. Well, have a good time tonight – and don't forget what Sister Ambrose said, if he parks the car in a lonely lane start to sing a hymn!

(*All freeze momentarily – Joan on the 'phone, Declan waiting for the outcome, Nuala on the 'phone, Alice wanting her to go and to stay.*)

(*Station jingle in hard, followed by Bobby Bold. Actors unfreeze and begin the next scene.*)

SCENE FIVE

(We see Declan waiting for Joan in DSC. Now we see Nuala: she crosses a street and goes to a telephone. Throughout this action we hear:)

BOBBY   *(station jingle)* That's it – the big one: Radio Active where we're heading up to lunch time and it's music all the way with me Bobby Bold, rocked but not rolled, starting with a million-seller from a few years back, and the time here on Radio Active is twenty-seven minutes before one.

(Neil Diamond's 'Beautiful Noise' begins. At the time check, Alice, Declan and Nuala check their watches. Declan and Nuala pause to adjust theirs. Then 'Beautiful Noise' fades out and:)

BOBBY   Sorry about that time-check, should have been twenty-*three* minutes before one.

(As 'Beautiful Noise' is brought-up again, Declan and Nuala angrily re-adjust their watches. Nuala then enters the 'phone-box and dials. Joan rushes to meet Declan, silently apologises. They both angrily indicate their watches. They kiss and go. As the 'phone rings in Alice's house, the music fades to out.)

ALICE   *(answering the 'phone)* Mrs Alice Ryan speaking.

NUALA   *(in Bogart accent)* Okay blue-eyes, now here's the plan – and I don't want any slip-up ya hear, or you could find yourself at the bottom of the river in a pair of concrete slippers.

ALICE   *(mock horror)* Nuala! Would you stop that cod-acting on the telephone.

NUALA   *(Bogart still)* I'm down-town here at Roberts Café and I want you to put on your glad-rags and get your ass down here fast.

ALICE   Nuala, will you not be imitating that Humpy Bogart.

NUALA   *(normal voice)* It's Humphrey, Mother. Right: I'm going to have lunch at Roberts so why don't you come along and we'll eat together?

ALICE   Eat at Roberts? But why, Nuala – why can't we eat here like we do every day.

NUALA   *Because* we eat there every day! Look Mother, if you don't . . . .

ALICE   And you want us to be giving Mr Roberts money for serving us food? To be keeping his restaurant open for him when we can . . . .

NUALA   (*loudly*) And I have something important to tell you.

ALICE   Oh, there's nothing wrong, is there?

NUALA   Oh no, there's nothing wrong, Mother.

ALICE   You didn't get the job on the newspaper, did you.

NUALA   Not telling – until you show up here at Roberts.

ALICE   If it's something important why can't you tell me now. It's silly, Nuala, for us to be going out when I can get a perfectly good meal here. Who'll be down there anyway?

NUALA   Oh, no one Mother . . . (*Bogart accent*) . . . unless you start to sing to the fuzz. So, follow the instructions, blue-eyes and nothing will happen. Roberts at one o'clock, okay? And if we like it, maybe we can play it again . . . Sam.

ALICE   Nuala . . . Nuala, I don't want . . . .

(*Nuala puts the 'phone down, moves off. Alice replaces the receiver, not too happy. Now, as Radio Active is heard, Alice puts on a hat, scarf and coat.*)

BOBBY   That was one from our vinyl vaults, gone from the charts but not from our hearts, here on, Radio Active the Station that cares about you. It's fast approaching one o'clock and I'm glad to say it's nice out, so don't believe Super Tramp when they tell you that . . . .

(*We hear "It's Raining Again" by Super Tramp and fade as:*)

SCENE SIX

(*Roberts Restaurant: downstage centre area. Nuala and Alice have just sat down. Alice very uncomfortable*)

ALICE   I don't like these restaurants, Nuala – and I don't know anyone who does this in the middle of the day.

NUALA   Well – we're being different then. That's good.

ALICE   The only time I was ever here before was with your Father at the County Council Dinner. And all his friends in the Council were here then – *and* it was at night.

NUALA   And you don't want to hear my news?

ALICE   (*suddenly relaxed*) Your news? Oh, of course I do. You didn't really get the job on the newspaper, did you? Oh, with your qualification from Dublin you'll be great in . . . .

NUALA   No, Mother.

ALICE   (*pause*) 'No, you wouldn't be great' or 'No you didn't get the newspaper job'?

NUALA   No – I didn't even *apply* for the newspaper job.

ALICE   But I thought you were going to . . . .

NUALA   I applied to the Radio Station. Radio Active.

ALICE   You applied to work with pirates?   But what are you . . .?

NUALA   Their ad was for a newsreader and magazine presenter. So I sent in this fabulous application *and* a demo.

ALICE   (*lost*) A what?

NUALA   A demo. A demo tape. You know, I read some stuff onto a cassette, bit of chat and that, and sent it to them. So they'd know how I sounded. That's a demo.

ALICE   I thought a demo was a class of a riot.

(*Declan and Joan now move across the restaurant, to leave. Joan will see Alice, but not pretend. Nuala will see Joan but not pretend. There will, therefore, be a moment of embarrassing indecision as:*)

NUALA   Well, it could be a class of riot when they hear it. (*To Alice, of Joan*) Oh there's . . . Mother, don't *look*!

JOAN   (*softly to Declan*)   Don't look – there's Nuala and her . . . .

DECLAN   (*turning*) Where?

ALICE   (*to Nuala, turning*) Who?

JOAN   (*to Declan*) I said don't look!

NUALA   (*to Alice*) Oh Mother, I said not to . . . . !

ALICE   (*too late*) Oh . . . hello . . . Declan, how are you?

DECLAN   (*too late*) Mrs . . . Ryan.
NUALA   Declan.

(*Now all pretence is replaced by enthusiasm.*)

JOAN   Ah Nuala! I didn't see you there! And Mrs Ryan!
NUALA   Joan! I thought it was you but . . . eh . . . .

(*Awkward silence. Joan and Nuala begin to speak at the same time and stop. Then:*)

JOAN   We were just heading back – we usually eat here together, it's close to Declan's building site.
ALICE   Oh, are you finished your electrical apprenticeship?
DECLAN   (*laughs*) Have my own little business now, Mrs Ryan.
JOAN   Declan is in charge of all the electrical installation in the new housing estate – out in Harwood Heights. Including our new home.
NUALA   I'll bet you'll do a good job on that one, Declan.
DECLAN   There'll be switches everywhere, Nuala. (*to Joan*) Including one for the electric blanket . . . .
JOAN   Declan! Will you stop!
ALICE   That's grand. My daughter Carol in California is often asking after you, Declan – she'll be delighted to hear you're doing so well.
DECLAN   Oh Carol and I were great friends, (*to Nuala*) that's when you were just a small freckle-face, Nuala, playing with your dolls.
JOAN   Oh, Nuala is now a qualified journalist.
NUALA   Looking for a job.
ALICE   (*softly to Nuala*) Ah Nuala, what did you want to say that for.

(*Short embarrassed silence.*)

JOAN   Well, well I better be heading back to my solicitor . . . .
ALICE   And Declan to his houses . . . ?
DECLAN   Oh yeah . . . it's all go . . . .
JOAN   (*to Nuala*) We must have that drink sometime, Nuala – I'll give you a buzz.

NUALA   That'd be lovely, Joan.
DECLAN   Nice to see you again, Nuala, Mrs Ryan.
ALICE   Goodbye Declan.
JOAN   (*quietly to Nuala*) Listen you won't be in the way or anything – he won't mind.
NUALA   Thanks . . . well . . . .
JOAN   Okay. Goodbye Mrs Ryan.
ALICE   Goodbye, love.

(*Joan and Declan leave.*)

NUALA   Oh anyway, Mother, as I was saying . . . .
ALICE   How old is Joan now?
NUALA   Oh, Mother, before we start to go through all that again – she is still the same age as I am.
ALICE   They're so attentive to each other. Would you not like to know a nice lad like Declan now?
NUALA   I know plenty of nice lads like Declan.
ALICE   I know, Nuala, but would you not like to be going out like Joan.
NUALA   You mean having lunch in here together, and going shopping together . . . .
ALICE   (*enthusiastically*) Yes!
NUALA   . . . and then getting engaged together and buying a house together and choosing furniture together . . . .
ALICE   Oh yes – exactly!
NUALA   No, Mother – I wouldn't.
ALICE   You wouldn't? (*pause*) Oh now, I'm sure there were some grand lads up in Dublin who . . . .
NUALA   The grand lads up in Dublin have nothing to do with it, Mother.
ALICE   Then what is it?
NUALA   Well, for starters, I'm still only twenty-two . . . .
ALICE   Ah sure Joan is only twenty-two and look at her.
NUALA   Yes, but that's Joan.
ALICE   When *I* was twenty-two, I was already married to your father and . . . .
NUALA   (*testily*) And that's how you came to depend so much on him . . . .
ALICE   (*testily*) That's how it should be, Nuala. We all need

	someone to depend on . . . .
NUALA	(*sharply*) Except when we don't have them anymore, we're suddenly lost!
ALICE	(*pause, quietly*) I'm not lost, Nuala.
NUALA	(*quietly*) No, Mother, of course you're not lost – and neither am I. And that's why I'm telling you about my interview. for the Radio Station.
ALICE	Interview? You never said anything about an interview. You said you sent in an application and a . . . a . . . deemo . . . .
NUALA	A demo, yes – but my real news is that they have called me for an interview.
NUALA	And sure why wouldn't they call you for an interview? Not only call you, but give you the job – and you with your qualifications from Dublin, and your grand speaking voice and all . . . .
NUALA	I know, Mother, don't tell me – tell them!
ALICE	And when is it – this interview?
NUALA	Next Wednesday. (*takes a letter from her bag*) At ten o'clock in the morning with a Mr Sean Delaney – whoever he may be. Here's the letter he sent.
ALICE	(*looks at the letter*) Now, please God. (*pause*) If you were on the radio all the time, the fellows would be beating a right path to your door. You'd be like a film star. You'd have one in no time . . . a grand lad . . . .
NUALA	(*laughs*) Only one, Mother?
ALICE	(*laughs*) Well, one for a start anyway. (*mock seriousness*) Do you hear what you have me saying, Nuala Ryan!

SCENE SEVEN

(*We hear Radio Active*)

JUSTIN	(*Station jingle*) That's it 459, sweet as wine. And now, a word for the wise from Radio Active's good guys: people can tell a lot about you from your appearance – so, take it from Justin Day, a little elegance goes a long way.

Whether you're dressing for that late date, that coffee morning or, very important, *that vital interview*, the way you look could be your passport to Paradise. Okay and here's a golden oldie from George McCrea. It went into the Charts on June 29th, 1974, and stayed there for fourteen baby-rocking weeks.

(Fifteen seconds of 'Rock Your Baby' and fade. Bobby Bold, aged 36, rather too flashily groomed and dressed, enters. He sits at a desk in DSC area. Nuala enters for her interview).

BOBBY   Ah, *(looks at his papers)* Nuala Ryan, is it?

NUALA   Yes, that's right.

BOBBY   Ah, thanks for coming in – I'm Sean Delaney. *(shakes hands)* Sit down there now.

NUALA   Thank you, Mr. Delaney.

BOBBY   I have . . . I've heard your demo– thanks for sending it in – it's good, very good, I like it . . . a lot.

NUALA   Thank you.

BOBBY   And you have qualifications. I see from . . . ?

NUALA   Oh yes – I qualified from the College of Journalism in Dublin.

BOBBY   Oh – so you worked on some of the Dublin newspapers then, did you?

NUALA   Well – not in a permanent capacity. I was doing a lot of freelance work for the Dublin dailies and for some magazines and I had a regular slot in a community paper, but some time ago my father died and I had to come back.

BOBBY   And how long will you be back for . . . be *here* for?

NUALA   For some time, I should think.

BOBBY   *(searching)* You're married in Dublin, are you?

NUALA   No – I came back to look after my mother, as a matter of fact. You see she lives alone now.

BOBBY   *(relieved)* Ah, I see. Good. *(notes this)* Now tell me, Nuala, are you familiar with Radio Active a'tall? Have you heard any of our programmes?

NUALA   Yes I have. I enjoy the station very much.

BOBBY   Good. Well we've been going about three months – we're teething, as you might say – and, at present, we're mainly into a music and chat format. It's working well for us – we have three main D.J.'s there's myself, Justin Day and . . . Wolfman Moses.

NUALA   And . . . Bobby Bold?

BOBBY   Bobby Bold? (*pause*) Bobby Bold – that's me. I'm Bobby Bold. Well, I'm really Sean Delaney – but Bobby Bold on Radio Active. Justin Day is really Eamonn McGovern – and now I suppose you want to know who Wolfman Moses really is?

NUALA   Well I was beginning to wonder . . . .

BOBBY   (*laughs*) I don't know who the blazes he is. I met him once when the station opened, and all I could get out of him was that his name really was Moses. But he's good, the listeners like him and that's what counts. (*seriously*) Anyway, that's our present personnel line-up. Alright?

NUALA   Yes.

BOBBY   Now, what I need, Nuala – to attract the ads and the listeners – is a female voice on the station. In my estimation we need news bulletins and, if all goes well, a Magazine Programme in the evening for the kids: advice, questions, items of interest and so forth. Alright?

NUALA   Yes, that sounds very interesting.

BOBBY   Now . . .(*looks at his papers*) . . . I can make no promises at this stage – I do have other applicants to interview – but with the News section, would you see yourself taking the news from the local newspapers or . . . . ?

NUALA   Well yes – but I think we should have our own sources in local areas. I mean, I don't think we should take copy from just the national dailies or RTE, but we should have our own leads, to interest our own listeners and, indeed, have stringers in certain local communities.

BOBBY   Eh . . . stringers?

NUALA   Yes.

BOBBY   Oh yes. (*writes quickly*) Stringers.

NUALA   I think that our image in the News Department should be quite recognisable and . . . well, individual.

BOBBY   (*still writing*) Exactly. We must be individual. Now, how are your music tastes, Nuala? Do you like all that Heavy Metal stuff?

NUALA   Some of it, yes. I think I have fairly wide tastes in music.

BOBBY   Good. Well, we have a top-class record library at the station – from the current singles to the oldies in our Vinyl Vaults. Now – any immediate thoughts, Nuala, on the Magazine Programme . . . .?

NUALA   Well, I think a Magazine Programme could be very challenging: I mean, I think there's great potential in local and community radio to . . . well, as McLuhan puts it: 'Let the medium be the message'!

BOBBY   (*impressed*) 'Let the medium be the message'! Of course.

NUALA   There are many social issues that I feel could be presented in a balanced way with good incisive interviewing, and perhaps some major issues. We could invite members of the local community in to use the station . . . .

BOBBY   . . . and plenty of rock and roll in between.

NUALA   (*quietly*) Yes.

BOBBY   (*pause*) Now, Nuala, money. Whether I appoint you or not . . . eh . . . you must understand that all of this is very experimental and dependant on the listeners' reaction *and* the advertisers, what we're talking about in terms of money is a four-week trial period of say . . . £60 per week? How does that sound to you?

NUALA   Yes, that seems reasonable, Mr Delaney, for the trial period.

BOBBY   Good. Eh, now your name – how would you feel about changing it?

NUALA   Changing it?

BOBBY   (*thoughtfully*) Oh, maybe it's okay: plenty of rhyming possibilities – 'Nuala Ryan on 459' or 'Feelin' fine with Nuala Ryan' . . . (*laughs, to Nuala*) Well, that's it . . . eh . . . Nuala – unless you have some questions for me?

NUALA   No, I don't think there's anything else . . . .

BOBBY   Well, I have your home number here, so I can contact you there one way or the other.

NUALA   Yes, of course.

BOBBY   Nice to meet you, Nuala.

NUALA   Thank you.

BOBBY   Bye-bye now.

NUALA   Goodbye.

SCENE EIGHT

(*Radio Active is immediately heard*)

W MOSES   (*howls*) This is Wolfman Moses, rising from his bed of blood-red roses here on Radio Active, calling all you wolves and she-wolves (*howls*). And be careful tonight all you young lovers – Wolfman Moses sees everything . . . my eyes are burning red into the night and my fangs are glistening white – so stay close together, young lovers and speak gently to each other because Wolfman Moses is on the midnight prowl. Now, listen to this, all you who are deep in love:

(*Fifteen seconds of 'Romeo and Juliet' by Dire Straits and fade. Declan and Joan are in downstage left area – Joan's house*)

DECLAN   Now you are being totally unreasonable, Joan.

JOAN   *I'm* being unreasonable?! My birthday is only once a year and this is the first year *we're engaged* for it – and now you say you can't go to the concert . . . you're telling me you can't go . . . .

DECLAN   Ah Joan come on . . . .

JOAN   *Two* days before it you come over here and tell me you can't go – after I telling everyone that we *are* going! What am I supposed to tell them now? What will they all think?

DECLAN   Tell them the truth – I'm working overtime.

JOAN   Ah, what do they care about your overtime – how often do we get a chance to go up to a Chris De Burgh concert in Dublin? How often, Declan?

DECLAN   Look – he'll be on again and we'll go. That's a promise. Okay?

JOAN   No, it's not okay.

DECLAN   But why? He lives in Dublin now so he'll . . . .

JOAN   Because it won't be my birthday, that's why. Because you promised me that concert for my birthday and . . . .

DECLAN   But your birthday isn't even the night of his concert.

JOAN   Ah, don't make excuses, Declan. You promised me that concert as a birthday present and I'm after telling the whole town . . . .

DECLAN (*now angry*) And now I'm telling you that I have to work overtime.

JOAN Oh, very convenient, Declan – on the one night that I asked you to take me . . . .

DECLAN It's not very convenient – it's bloody inconvenient! But we need the money!

JOAN We need it that badly, do we? That we can't go up to Dublin for one night?

DECLAN Yes we do need it that badly – that is if we want to get married!

JOAN I sometimes wonder about that, Declan.

DECLAN About what?

JOAN You wanting to get married?

DECLAN Of course I want to get married – I'm bloody engaged, amn't I? Jeez . . . .

JOAN (*pause, quietly*) Anyway, what about the tickets then?

DECLAN (*quietly*) What tickets?

JOAN For the concert. If you paid for them and we're not going, that's a waste of money, surely?

DECLAN It isn't – I haven't paid for them yet.

JOAN But you told me last week that you *had* paid for them!

DECLAN I said I booked them.

JOAN You said you paid for them.

DECLAN I booked them, Joan – not paid for them.

JOAN You told me you paid for those tickets.

DECLAN I never said that.

JOAN More lies, Declan.

DECLAN They're not lies! If you'd only open your bloody ears.

JOAN (*nervous laugh*) You know, Declan, I don't think I could seriously marry someone who is so . . . so careless with the truth.

DECLAN Then don't Don't bloody-well marry me!

JOAN What do you mean by that, Declan Murray?

DECLAN (*pause*) Ah Joan. (*he takes her in his arms*) Joan, why are we fighting like this? Why? (*she eventually puts her arms around him*).

SCENE NINE

(*The 'phone immediately rings in Alice Ryan's house. Alice and Nuala are there.*)

ALICE   (*into 'phone*) Mrs Alice Ryan speaking. (*pause*) Hold the line please. (*to Nuala*) It's a man.

NUALA   (*into 'phone*) Oh . . . yes, of course. (*pause*) Oh. (*pause*) Oh yes, I understand. (*pause*) Yes. (*pause*) And thank you very much for calling. Goodbye.

ALICE   (*pause*) Who was that?

NUALA   (*sadly*) The radio station.

ALICE   Oh? (*pause*) And?

NUALA   (*suddenly*) I got the job!

ALICE   You didn't!

NUALA   I did. I'm going to work for Radio Active!

(*We hold Nuala and Alice in a five-second freeze – hugging each other.*)

(*Over this the full sound of ABBA's 'Super Trouper' on Radio Active is heard on all speakers – and the studio set is revealed. Nuala walks up towards it.*)

(*Bobby Bold, cans on ears, silently welcomes her, ushering her in as he prepares to cue a record. He is on the air.*)

(*Nuala looks around in quiet amazement – at a cardboard box marked 'Vinyl Vault', at old pop posters, old chairs, a church calendar on the wall, full ash-trays, general tattiness.*)

BOBBY   (*into mike*) That was ABBA and this is Bobby Bold, rocked but not rolled here on the big one, Radio Active 459 and feelin' fine, the station that cares about *you*. It's a good day out, but cold. At three o'clock, in four minutes time, it's that Dedicated Follower of Fashion, Mr Elegant Justin Day and Justin will be bringing you good sounds and good advice until seven. Now, hear this, all you guys out there – from next Monday Radio Active will bring you the delightful, delectable Nuala

Ryan here on 459 (*winks at Nuala*). Nuala will be bringing you news, local and international, and all that's happening out there in the big bad world. Take it from me, guys, Nuala is nice – and waiting to hear from . . . *you*. Okay, it's me, it's Bobby Bold, rocked but not rolled, taking you up to Justin Day-time at three with The Human League and 'Mirror Man' . . . .

(*Ten seconds of this record. Bobby takes the cans from his ears, turns down the sound. Now he speaks normally.*)

BOBBY Oh, great to see you, Nuala – well, what do you think?

NUALA Well, I think . . . .

BOBBY I know – all a bit strange at first, but you'll soon find your way around. Now, the Vinyl Vaults are . . . (*looks around, picks up the carton*) . . . the Vinyl Vaults are here. We have the Chart singles, Nuala, over here (*another carton*) and there's some special records down here, we play them every hour – it's the promotion of a record company I have an interest in, but don't say anything to Justin about that. Now, here's the turntable . . . .

NUALA Oh yes. This is your treble and fade, is it? (*points*)

BOBBY Oh – got it all at college, eh? Now the jingle tapes are here, Advertiser lists are here and their tapes are there. Oh, time signals are very important – so there's the clock.

(*The 'phone rings*)

BOBBY Oh, it could be reaction to you already. (*D.J. accent into 'phone*) Bobby Bold, rocked but not rolled, on Radio Active. (*pause, normal accent*) Two side-loin chops, is it love, half a pound of mince, and a pint of milk. Oh, do you want me to get the Farley's Rusks? Okay, love that's grand. (*pause*) Bye-bye. (*replaces 'phone, to Nuala*) Ah . . . domestic. Now, where was I . . .

NUALA (*looks at her watch*) Surely the elegant Justin Day should be here by now – it's nearly one minute to three . . . .

BOBBY Don't you ever believe that *he'll* be late. His whole life is

one big, boring timetable. He lives below in the
basement, and he has it all timed to the second. Now, the
toilet is out there, the kettle is there and for God's sake
don't leave any scraps of food about the place, Wolfman
Moses has a hamster in here at night.

NUALA   Really? (*pause*) And I begin with the news at one on
Monday, Mr Delaney?

BOBBY   Sean is the name. Listen, I have the roster all set out for
you here, Nuala. (*gives Nuala a sheet of paper*) You'll be
reading the News at . . . one, three-thirty, five and the
Magazine Programme from seven to eight. Now, twenty
seconds, (*laughs*) . . . watch that door for the arrival of
our beautiful Mr Elegant.

(*Bobby puts on the cans. Sits at the turntables. Fades music.*)

BOBBY   (*into mike*) 'The Human League' here and now, coming
up to three, I see that Dedicated Follower of Fashion,
Mr Elegant, Mr Justin Day, coming sweeping into the
Studio. Hi Justin. I'll tell you, girls, he's looking good
today, white suit and pink carnation and he's got the
music, the chat, advice and all that, ready to keep you
fine here on 459. But now, it's me, it's Bobby Bold,
rocked but not rolled . . . .

(*At this point, as Bobby talks on, Justin Day enters through the door.
He is 25, un-shaven, lank oily hair, old sweater and jeans, one tennis
shoe – very dirty and un-washed. He has a tubercular cough that he
stifles with a handkerchief. He carries records and pop magazines.
He first checks the church calendar and then puts on the cans and sits
beside Bobby.*)

BOBBY   . . . saying goodbye and reminding you that Radio Active
is the station that cares about you, the station that not
only brings you the best sounds around but, from next
Monday, News local and international from the delightful and delectable Nuala Ryan here on 459. And now at
three o'clock on the dot I'm handing you over to Mr
Elegant, Justin Day. My, my, Justin, you *are* looking
sexy today.

JUSTIN   (*into mike*) Looking good and feeling good too Bobby – on top of the world, the healthy mind in the healthy body. (*turns to cough into his handkerchief as Bobby continues*).

BOBBY   And I bet you've got words to the wise from the Radio Active good guys?

JUSTIN   Sure I have, Bobby – and advice for any of you troubled out there and well, I can't say it often enough: the way you look tells a lot about the way you are.

BOBBY   You've said it, Mr Elegance. But I gotta go: Bobby Bold, rocked but not rolled, movin' on.

JUSTIN   Thanks for a great show, Bobby – it'll take a good man to beat it . . . .

BOBBY   . . . but it won't take him long!

JUSTIN   There he goes, gang – off to meet the latest girl of his dreams – they don't call him Bold for nothing.

BOBBY   Ho-ho-ho.

JUSTIN   · . . but I'm Justin Day, your Dedicated Follower of Fashion and today, gang, is the Feast of the Beheading of St John the Baptist – okay, you guys, don't knock it if you haven't tried it – it's a Justin Day Feast-Day. And now to start the show it's three in a row from The Police.

(*We hear the beginning of 'Walking on the Moon'. Bobby then silently motions to Justin to meet Nuala. Justin turns down the sound and comes over. He is very introverted, off the mike*)

BOBBY   (*to Justin*) Meet our new D.J. and Newscaster, Nuala Ryan. Nuala, Eamonn McGovern.

NUALA   I'm pleased to meet you, Eamonn.

JUSTIN   Nuala – short for Fionnuala, yes?

NUALA   Yes, that's right.

JUSTIN   (*disappointed*) No Feast-Day for Fionnuala – she was pre-Christian. You have a second name, no?

NUALA   Oh yes, I do. (*pause, quietly*) It's Brigid.

JUSTIN   (*delighted*) Brigid! Great! St. Brigid – Feast-Day 1st February! Patroness of Ireland!

NUALA   That's very good.

BOBBY   (*cutting*) He's good at everything except washing himself. (*to Justin*) I suppose you left that place below looking like a pig-sty.

JUSTIN It's okay.

BOBBY Well you'll have to shape-up now that we have a lady here. (*to Nuala*) Listen, I'm nipping over to the Super-market. I've got to get some stuff for the wife, anything you want to know about the place, ask him. Don't worry you'll be grand. (*to Justin, cutting*) I don't suppose I can get you anything – a bar of soap or a packet of razor blades?

JUSTIN (*annoyed*) No.

BOBBY No. (*brightly, to Nuala*) I'll see you later, Nuala.

NUALA And thanks very much for everything, Sean.

(*Bobby Bold goes. Awkward moment.*)

NUALA I loved your entrance – timed to the last second.

JUSTIN You think that time is important, no?

NUALA Oh yes – yes I do. I like to be on time.

JUSTIN Right – it's very important. Being late is the worst thing that can happen to you. I wouldn't be stuck here, in this place looking like this only I was late once . . . for something . . . a few years ago. You believe that, no?

NUALA Oh yes, yes I do, of course. (*pause*) Well, what were you late for . . . a few years ago?

JUSTIN A girl.

NUALA Oh.

JUSTIN But you know it'd bore you – yeah?

NUALA No – it wouldn't.

JUSTIN It bores the hell out of a lot of people – especially one old bastard. You know who I mean, yeah?

NUALA You don't mean that fellow who does the night show?

JUSTIN Oh, Wolfman Moses! Him! He *is* weird. No one ever sees him at all, but I hear him up here, howling half the night. And he has a big rat he feeds – it runs around everywhere. No, no – I don't mean him – I mean that old bastard Delaney, yeah?

NUALA Oh.

JUSTIN You . . . you going to be reading the News from Monday, yeah?

NUALA Yes. At one.

JUSTIN Journalist, yeah?

NUALA   Well, I trained as one in Dublin, yes.

JUSTIN And married, no?

NUALA   Do you always answer your own questions, Eamonn?

JUSTIN No. Do you think I do, yeah?

NUALA   Yes, I do. (*pause*) My turn is it? Well, do you really live downstairs in the basement?

JUSTIN Yeah, yeah I pay Delaney for it. And not married are you, no?

NUALA   No.

JUSTIN I nearly was. Once. In London. Only I was late. I just met her at this disco in Hammersmith on a Saturday night, said I'd see her at the corner of Perkins Tea Bar on Wednesday – you know Perkins Tea Bar in Hammersmith, no?

NUALA   No.

JUSTIN No. Said I'd see her there on the corner at eight. Forgot the time and when I got there the big clock on the corner said twenty-one minutes past and she was gone. You know where she was gone – no?

NUALA   No.

JUSTIN No, neither do I. But she was gone. I asked around, put ads in the paper, went back to the disco every night for three weeks. Nothing. Never saw her again. (*quietly*) Her name was Monica. Feast-Day 27th August. (*pause*) That's why I care about time – that's why no one should ever be late. She would've saved me. She was the only girl I ever knew who would've saved me. You can understand that, yeah?

NUALA   Oh yes, yes of course, Eamonn – but well, I mean, how well did you know her . . . I mean, if you only danced with her for one night and you never saw her after . . . .

JUSTIN You got a boyfriend, no?

NUALA   Well . . . not at the moment, actually.

JUSTIN (*politely*) Then you wouldn't understand. (*pause*) You eh . . . you religious, no?

NUALA   Well, I don't know all the feast-days like you . . . .

JUSTIN Saved me. Through drugs, drink, the hard stuff, the lot. But I made it. Completely, total one-hundred-per-cent . . . (*immediately coughs badly*) . . . recovery. Hang on

... (*now into mike*) Cutting in here kids to tell you all out there in Radio Active-land that your Mr Elegant, Justin Day is here with all the pop information at his well-manicured finger-tips. You got a question, on any subject, or a problem, or something nagging on your mind – then you can write me, and just send your pigeon winging in here through our panoramic studio windows, or, better still, hey, hey hey, you 'phone me here, now at 25145. Got that? It's 25145. Questions, problems or if you just want to chat. I'm here, to talk to you – Justin Day, just waiting . . . for *your* call now. 25145. Okay?

(*'Message in a Bottle' by The Police*)

(*We hold the 'phone, we hold the sound of the music. Justin is poised over the 'phone, waiting. It will never ring. He, embarrassed, indicates to Nuala that it is just a matter of time. Nuala looks around the studio.*)

SCENE TEN

(*Fade music. Now DSL area – Joan's house. Declan and Joan*)

JOAN   (*with an album*) You shouldn't have, Declan – it's the only Chris de Burgh I haven't got – you really shouldn't have gone to all the trouble.

DECLAN   Well, you *were* looking forward to the concert . . . .

JOAN   Yeah, but I still didn't expect you to buy me an album . . . (*looks at it*) . . . it's great.

DECLAN   Yeah, and the words are inside – so you can learn them now and not have to make up your own.

JOAN   Okay, I promise. You're very good, Declan. Thanks. (*kisses him lightly*)

DECLAN   And what was that supposed to be?

JOAN   What was what . . . ?

DECLAN   That was an L.P. I gave you – not a single! Do I have to buy the whole bloody record shop to get a decent kiss?

JOAN   (*laughs*) Oh. No, of course you don't, Declan. (*kisses him lovingly*)

DECLAN That's more like it, Mrs Murray. (*both laugh, sees the book of patterns*) Eh, what's this?

JOAN (*all enthusiasm*) Oh – I wanted you to see these, Declan – they're wallpaper patterns.

DECLAN Wallpaper patterns? It might be better if you waited until the walls were up.

JOAN They *are* practically up, Declan – and the man in Wallace's let me borrow these so we could look at them together.

DECLAN (*unenthusiastic*) Yeah, right.

JOAN (*indicates*) Look, I was thinking of this kind for the spare room – the one where you could put the pool table you were talking about.

DECLAN (*suddenly interested*) What? Oh yeah, that room – right, let's see. (*studies the pattern*) Yes, the colour is good – but it'd have to be really hard wearing, Joan – what with fellows lying up against it, leaning their cues on it, scratching it with chalk, you know.

JOAN But it does look really hard-wearing, Declan, doesn't it?

DECLAN Yeah.

JOAN (*turns page*) And look – for the lounge: that would match the dark-brown leather upholstery of that suite with the tip-up foot-rests . . . .

DECLAN (*agrees*) Yes, it would.

JOAN (*turns page*) And this one is nice, I think – this one. And it's plastic-coated for wiping off finger marks and stains . . . and I like the bright shades. (*a little tenderly*) Would be nice in the nursery.

DECLAN (*unenthusiastic*) Yeah, it would be alright. (*next page*) Ah jeez, look at the colours! Nuala Ryan's technicolour sweater.

JOAN Nuala? Have you seen her since?

DECLAN Saw her yesterday – coming across High Street. I needn't tell you I was gone like a flash.

JOAN Ah Declan – you should have gone over and talked to her.

DECLAN About what? About the College of Journalism? About writing for newspapers? About all her intellectual friends up in Dublin? No thanks!

JOAN   You know everytime I ask her if she went out with a boyfriend in Dublin all she ever says is that his name is Robert Redford.

DECLAN   Ah jeez, Robert Redford! That one has her sights set high alright.

JOAN   Ah no, Declan – I think it's only her way of covering-up. I don't think she's had a boyfriend at all – in fact, I don't think she even went out much with any friends up there.

DECLAN   Isn't she going to read the news or something on Radio Active soon?

JOAN   Yeah, on Monday – her first broadcast!

DECLAN   Yes, well that should bring her in plenty of new intellectual friends. There'll be no bloody standing her after that.

JOAN   Do you think she'll be very nervous? I'd be in bits if I had to do that.

DECLAN   I know you would – but it'd be no trouble to her. That one thinks she knows it all.

JOAN   (*pause*) Oh, Declan, you know those Deeds you signed for the house? Well . . . well I was told today that we both should have signed them. I don't suppose it matters, does it?

DECLAN   Are we back to Nuala Ryan again?

JOAN   What?

DECLAN   Was it her who told you that?

JOAN   No – as a matter of fact, it was Mr Moriarity.

DECLAN   Jeez, free advice from a solicitor! What else did he say?

JOAN   Ah, nothing else. He just mentioned that in passing.

DECLAN   And that's how it ought to be mentioned – it's only a technicality. If I dropped dead tomorrow . . . .

JOAN   . . . ah Declan, don't say that . . . .

DECLAN   No, but if I did – you'd have the house anyway. And that's a fact. Ask anyone. (*teases*) Even the great Nuala Ryan knows that.

JOAN   Hey Declan. (*pause*) Will we listen to her on Monday – just to see how she gets along?

DECLAN   I've a better idea.

JOAN   What's that?

DECLAN   Something more immediate – how about us listening to Chris de Burgh on your stereo. That'd be better than waiting for Nuala Ryan to hit the airwaves.

JOAN   (*laughs*) I'm not arguing. Come on – we'll put on side-two first– that has 'Borderline' on it.

DECLAN   Yeah, okay.

JOAN   (*as she goes*) Oh, you can take that book of patterns home with you if you like. (*goes*)

DECLAN   What? Oh yeah, I must. (*picks it up; goes after Joan*)

SCENE ELEVEN

(*Lights up on Alice Ryan's house, DSR area. Alice is speaking on the 'phone*)

ALICE   (*into 'phone*) 459 metres, Mary, it is near where Radio Éireann used to be. (*pause*) She's delighted. (*pause*) Oh, like her father, God rest him, wanting to take on the whole world single-handed and listen to nobody. (*pause*) Well, she's a little bit nervous, but I hear her practising all the time. (*pause*) Oh, that's right, and the News is full of those big foreign words so a prayer or two won't go astray . . . .

(*Lights up now on the studio where Nuala is nervously rehearsing her reading of the News*)

NUALA   (*reads*) . . . when the Irish Congress of Trade Unions . . . (*falters, coughs, tries again*) . . . When the Irish Congress of Trade Unions sanctioned the strike action by ten thousand . . . (*stops, corrects*); . . . by one hundred thousand employees in the public sector. A spokesman for the *Irish* Conf . . . (*stops, corrects*) . . . A spokesman for the Irish *Conference* of Professional and Service Associations . . . .

ALICE   (*continuing into 'phone*) . . . No, Nuala is making a recording of it, the whole news, so we can send a demo out to Carol in California. (*pause*) A demo. The tape it's called a demo. (*pause*) Ah, sure 'tis wonderful. (*pause*) Ah, the only pity of it is poor Joe isn't alive to hear it.

> (*pause*) Ah, that's right, Mary – 459 metres, we'll keep our fingers crossed. (*pause*) God bless now.

(*An immediate I.D. of Radio Active is heard followed by their new jingle for the News and the reporting sounds of telex. It is the day of Nuala's first broadcast.*

In the studio, Justin stands behind Nuala. Throughout her reading, Justin is nervous – but his mute confidence is evidenced as she expertly proceeds.

Lights still on Alice Ryan in her room listening. Also now on Joan and Declan in DSL with their transistor, listening.)

NUALA   (*reads confidently*) Good afternoon. This is Nuala Ryan at the Radio Active News Desk. It was confirmed this morning that negotiations to avert next week's one-day bus strike have broken down. A spokesman for the NBU accused CIE of what he called 'total intransigence in negotiation'. CIE had earlier said that they 'had hoped for a more realistic bargaining outlook'. but if the strike takes place it will leave the country without buses from midnight on Wednesday. (*pause*) The Irish Meat Exporters Association has announced that it is to complain to the EEC Commission for Agriculture about the Government's failure to implement the Community's Disease Eradication Scheme. On the International scene, the twelve-day truce in the Lebanon was threatened today when Israeli planes shot down a Syrian MG-25 over the town of Juniah. Israel has accused Syria of violating air space while Palestinian Radio has described the shooting as an act of unpardonable aggression. And, finally, in the USSR a chewing-gum has been discovered that is said to kill the craving for cigarettes. Claimed to be both pleasant-tasting and relaxing it has, however, only been tested on chimpanzees. Chain-smokers all! And that is all from me, Nuala Ryan at the News Desk of Radio Active. The time is now four minutes past one. News again at three-thirty. (*the Radio Active jingle is heard followed by 'The Theme from Harry's Game' by Clannad*)

(*Lights out on Declan and Joan. Alice Ryan proudly turns off the radio and sits back and plays Patience. In the studio, Bobby Bold enters carrying a radio-cassette.*)

JUSTIN   Oh . . . oh, that was magic . . . the greatest ever . . . far, far out . . . really blew my mind.

BOBBY   That sounded really great, Nuala . . . better than you'd hear on RTE – or the BBC for that matter.

NUALA   I think I pronounced 'Juniah' wrongly. It should have been 'Jun*i*ah'.

JUSTIN   I didn't notice that . . . .

BOBBY   It was perfect . . . .

JUSTIN   I'd've noticed it because I hear everything. No, no, no, it was wonderful . . . it was beautiful . . . .

BOBBY   There'll be plenty of reaction, plenty of reaction, believe me, in letters and on the 'phone.

JUSTIN   And you got the time exactly right.

BOBBY   People will be ringing in . . . .

JUSTIN   Hey, I think you must have done it before, no?

BOBBY   It's exactly what I wanted and I loved the ending with the chimps . . . the light-hearted ending is great . . . .

(*The 'phone rings*)

BOBBY   Oh! What did I tell you? Reaction already! (*picks up the 'phone*) Radio Active News Desk. (*pause*) A big carton of Weetabix, is it? (*pause*) A packet of Ariel and two heads of lettuce. (*pause*) And Pampers. (*pause*) Okay. Grand. Bye-bye. (*puts the 'phone down; to Nuala*) Domestic.

JUSTIN   (*to Nuala*) Domestic. (*Bobby Bold reacts in silent anger*).

NUALA   Sean . . . Sean, for the three-thirty news, I was thinking of doing yesterday's Farmers' Protest as a lead. It's local and I do have an individual report on it . . . .

BOBBY   Whatever you say, Nuala. Now, can we talk about the Magazine Programme you're doing tonight. What's it on? We need a good one to start.

JUSTIN   (*to Nuala*) You could do it on time-keeping, yeah. What happens when people are late. I once knew this girl in London . . . her name was Monica . . . and she'd've changed my life, only I . . . .

BOBBY   Will you shut-up! I am talking to Nuala! (*to Nuala*) Now, what had you in mind exactly?

NUALA   Well, I thought we'd deal with the facilities for young people in the area, and then if reaction was good, do a Special on job opportunities for young people. You know, how effective the AnCO courses and Youth Employment Schemes are. In fact, Sean, I thought we could do a Special each week on a particular topic?

BOBBY   Yes – I like it . . . .

JUSTIN   (*to Nuala*) Or drugs, yeah? I could give you all my personal details on glue-sniffing, smoking grass, pumping heroin . . . .

BOBBY   (*shouts angrily to Justin*) Will you kindly shut-up while I get things organised around here. In fact, get down to that dirty little hovel of yours and stay there until it's your programme time. Will you do that for me, McGovern, will you?

(*Justin fearfully retreats from the studio*)

BOBBY   (*calmly to Nuala*) No, I like that idea, Nuala, something good to get us started, something to get the programme off the ground. But we don't want to get too heavy, no attention from the Department of Posts and Telegraphs or that. No, just take it as it goes. (*puts the cans on; into the mike*) Oh yes, thank you Clannad and thank you Nuala Ryan at the News Desk, and what did I tell you guys, she's delightful and delectable and, tonight at seven, you can check-in for her very own Magazine Programme. It's a word to the wise from the Radio Active good guys – and now here's a Bobby Bold country classic.

(*We hold the music*)

SCENE TWELVE

(*In Alice's room. Alice with Joan*)

JOAN   Mammy just asked me to ask you, Mrs Ryan.

ALICE   Ah, that's very nice of her, but sure . . .

JOAN   . . . and Daddy did too.

ALICE   Ah, sure I know – they're a great partnership at the Bridge – but I couldn't play if my partner . . .

JOAN   Well, Mammy – and Daddy – think you should. She says the games haven't been the same without you.

ALICE   Ah well, it's Joe and I together who were the partnership. We won so many trophies and cups together and . . . .

JOAN   But . . . *you* could still go down and maybe . . . .

ALICE   (*brightly*) And sure maybe I will sometime. Sure I keep my hand in practice here playing this old Patience game . . . . (*pause*) Sit down there now and tell me, how is yourself and Declan getting along?

JOAN   Oh great. We were over looking at the house last week – well, it's not finished yet, but the gardens will be very big and the bay window will get the sun all through the afternoon . . . .

ALICE   Now, isn't that lovely . . . .

JOAN   (*great enthusiasm*) And . . . and in the summer we're going to have Barbecues on the patio, because Declan is going to fit in these beautiful lanterns and the garden will be all illuminated. And then at Christmas-time we're going to have these lovely fairy lights running from the back porch right down the lawn as far as the . . . (*stops, awkwardly*) Nuala is doing very well too, Mrs Ryan – we listen to her Magazine Programme every week now.

ALICE   Yes – but I'm sure some people don't like them too much.

JOAN   Ah, we think they're great.

ALICE   Do you?

JOAN   We liked the one on the travelling people; and the one last week on the youth clubs was really super . . . .

ALICE   Well now, Joan, between yourself and myself – I think that tonight she went a bit too far. I mean, naming

	people in the Government is not right.
JOAN	We didn't . . . we didn't hear tonight's. (*looks at her watch*) Mrs Ryan, I have to see Declan at half-ten . . . .
ALICE	And here am I keeping you talking. Thanks very much for calling down, love, and tell your mother I'll see her at the Bridge Club some other time.
JOAN	Okay, Mrs Ryan, I'll tell her that.
ALICE	And give my regards to Declan.
JOAN	I will, Mrs Ryan. 'Bye now.

(*Joan leaves the house. Alice goes to her radio. Joan meets Nuala outside, coming in*)

NUALA	Ah-ha!
JOAN	Oh, Nuala.
NUALA	(*laughs*) Don't tell me you're a night-prowler on the sly! Wait until Declan hears about this.
JOAN	(*laughs*) No. (*seriously*) My Ma asked me to ask your mother to go to the Bridge Club again.
NUALA	What did she say to that?
JOAN	Well, she said she'd go . . . sometime.
NUALA	Oh, I can just imagine when that would be!
JOAN	She's very proud of your radio programmes, Nuala – and we think they're great too.
NUALA	Yes, but you know sometimes it is difficult in there Joan, to know whether you're doing too much on any one subject or too little for that matter . . . .
JOAN	Yes, I suppose. Listen, Nuala I'm seeing Declan at half-ten . . . .
NUALA	You better go so and tell him I was asking for him.
JOAN	I will – and you must come for that drink sometime. You keep putting it off.
NUALA	I'll surprise you some night.
JOAN	Now listen, Nuala you won't be in the way or anything. Declan won't mind, honestly.
NUALA	Great. Well, goodnight Joan.
JOAN	'Night, Nuala.

(*Joan goes off. Nuala goes into the house. Alice is listening to Wolfman Moses on the radio. Nuala silently stands behind her*)

W MOSES   (*howls*) Yeah, this is Wolfman Moses in his bed of blood-red roses and when the moon slides behind the clouds, Wolfman Moses will be on the prowl. Yeah, Wolfman Moses will leave his lair at Radio Active and with blood-red eyes and teeth of shining white will come looking for you. Yes . . . you. You can't escape the Wolfman tonight – but you could be spared if you learn how to please him and howl . . . .

ALICE   Howl?!

W MOSES   Howl like all Wolfman Moses lovers. Yeah, now you be a Wolfman Moses lover and howl. (*howls*)

ALICE   (*blesses herself*) Oh merciful God.

W MOSES   Come on, howl. (*howls; evil laugh*) I liked that – and now some music that Wolfman Moses knows you all . . . thirst . . . for . . . .

(*We hear Kate Bush: 'Wuthering Heights'*)

NUALA   (*suddenly*) Hello Mother.

ALICE   (*jumps*) Oh Nuala – Oh God, you gave me a fright. I thought you were that . . . .

NUALA   (*tenderly*) You thought I was Wolfman Moses, did you?

ALICE   Oh, what in the name of God, *is* he at all?

NUALA   I've no idea.

ALICE   But you must have seen him at the radio station.

NUALA   No one ever sees him. He comes in at ten when we're gone and Justin is downstairs in bed – and he leaves at three in the morning. Justin only hears him slamming the door. He keeps a hamster.

ALICE   Justin does?

NUALA   No – Wolfman Moses. Justin thinks it's a rat. But it's a hamster because Moses feeds it on Sunflower Seeds (*laughs*) and he howls . . . all night.

ALICE   Oh, it's no laughing matter, Nuala. You should sprinkle holy water around that studio. I've a little bottle of Knock water, you can bring it in with you.

NUALA   Mother – he's harmless.

ALICE   Well now, I wouldn't like to meet him on a dark night.

NUALA   Not much danger of you meeting anyone on a dark night – when you never go out.

ALICE   I'll go out – when I have something to go out to. Don't you be worrying about me.

NUALA   But you've just refused to go out to Bridge.

ALICE   Who told you that!

NUALA   Joan. I met her.

ALICE   Yes. Well, imagine me going up there on my own.

NUALA   And what's wrong with that?

ALICE   Oh, you don't know what it's like Nuala, to appear at Bridge on your own. I've seen it happen. It's an embarrassment for everyone concerned – looking for a partner for you . . . looking for someone else on their own.

NUALA   Mother, I'm sure that's an exaggeration.

ALICE   It's not an exaggeration Nuala – I'm not used to being without a partner. I'm not used to being on my own.

NUALA   Oh, Mother. Look, I miss Daddy too – I miss him very much. It's not easy for me without him either, but we've got to try and keep going. Daddy wouldn't have wanted you to be sitting here every day just . . . .

ALICE   But I'm grand here now – don't be worrying about me. (*brightly*) I might go out to Carol in California.

NUALA   Oh Mother, don't give me that – you couldn't stand it in California when you went out with Daddy for just a holiday.

ALICE   It might be different now.

NUALA   California doesn't get different. Look Mother, why don't you go out to the choir – now you can't tell me you need a partner for that?

ALICE   Oh, I listened to your programme about Widows Pensions tonight.

NUALA   (*frustrated*) Mother, it wasn't about Widows Pensions – it was about their position in society and what they can do for themselves – and indeed what some of them won't do.

ALICE   Yes – well I don't think you should have mentioned the Minister though – after all your father was in the County Council and . . . .

NUALA   You've changed the subject, Mother. Now, listen to me – promise me you'll go out to the choir or to Bridge. Come on, Mother – promise.

ALICE   Do you know what I think you want to happen to me?

NUALA   (*impatiently*) What?

ALICE   (*smiles*) I think you want me to be caught by that Wolfman Moses.

NUALA   (*capitulates*) Oh Mother. Oh, he'd be the one to shake you up alright. (*laughs*) Oh, Wolfman Moses would be the boy for you!

SCENE THIRTEEN

(*It is noon. Bobby Bold is in the studio. There is a pile of letters lying around. We hear the station jingle, then:*)

BOBBY   (*into the mike; quickly*) Hi – this is Bobby Bold, rocked but not rolled, welcoming you to another day here on wonderful Radio Active, the station that cares about *you*. I'm here through until three, then it's the Justin Day Show until seven. Nuala Ryan will be on the line from seven to eight. I've got plenty of mail here before me, reaction to Nuala Ryan's Magazine Programme and you keep it coming. And coming up here on Radio Active, it's two-in-a-row from Madness.

(*We hold the music loud. Bobby opens a letter. Reads it. Is angered. Opens another. More anger. Lifts the 'phone. Dials. Turns down the sound as the 'phone rings in Alice Ryan's house. As Alice answers the 'phone, Nuala walks into the studio.*)

ALICE   Mrs Alice Ryan speaking.

BOBBY   (*slams 'phone down; angrily, to Nuala*) I've been looking for you. Would you read that. (*gives Nuala a letter*)

NUALA   Oh – fan-mail and buckets of it.

BOBBY   Some fan-mail that is! It's about your bloody Widows Programme the other night.

ALICE   (*weakly into 'phone*) Mrs. Alice Ryan speaking. (*puts 'phone down; plays Patience*)

NUALA   (*reading*) Silly.

BOBBY   It is not silly. None of this is silly – they are serious letters from influential people. And I don't know what else is in the other stuff there addressed to you.

NUALA (*puts the letter down*) Well, I'll give them their say in tonight's programme. I'll read them out.

BOBBY Read them out? You will *not* read them out!

NUALA But why not, Sean? It's a serious issue, and they do have points of view.

BOBBY It's a bloody serious issue. Would you look, here's one letter from the Department of Social Welfare!

NUALA So what?

BOBBY So what? So, you've already attracted one Government Department to us – next it'll be the Post and Telegraphs – and that'll be the end of us. Closed down. No licence. Out on the street.

NUALA Sean, that's panic.

BOBBY It is not panic. You'll be on the dole, I'll be on the dole and McGovern will be on the dole. Now that may not worry you, but I have a wife and two kids to think about . . . .

NUALA But this reaction won't close the station, Sean – it will attract listeners. That's what we want. We want listeners and we get them by tackling social issues and evils, we get them by telling the truth about . . . .

BOBBY Stuff the truth, Nuala – we have the advertisers to think of.

NUALA (*angrily*) *And* listeners, Sean. Which comes first?

BOBBY Which what comes first?

NUALA Listeners come first. With listeners we get your advertis- ers. Look Sean, these letters represent listener reactions – from people who have been stirred-up enough to start writing. Now we are *doing* something on this station.

BOBBY Oh yes we are – we're wiping ourselves out: thanks to you!

NUALA We're not! We're dealing with important social issues!

BOBBY And I'm telling you now to forget about your important social issues – forget about your tinkers, forget about your widows, forget about all your . . . .

NUALA It's very hard for me to forget about the widows – I happen to live at home with one: my mother!

BOBBY And if you keep this up, she'll be living with someone on the dole! You'll be great company for each other: two important social issues sitting, looking at one another!

(*silence*)

NUALA So what do I do?

BOBBY You play the music. You read the news. You answer the questions. Do what I pay you to do. Leave the heavy stuff to the newspapers.

NUALA (*indicates the letters, quietly*) And just ignore these people, Sean. Ignore their points of view? Ignore reaction?

BOBBY To hell with reaction, Nuala. Just keep off the controversial stuff.

NUALA And what is 'controversial' supposed to mean?

BOBBY (*pause*) Look – just keep off it for the time being. Let this die down. Lie low for a while and when it settles, we'll see . . . we'll see how our advertisers have reacted. Then we'll be in a better position to judge. Right Nuala? Right? Right.

(*Nuala turns away. Bobby Bold puts on the cans and brings up the music: 'Our House' by Madness*)

SCENE FOURTEEN

(*Downstage centre area. A bar. Declan and Joan drinking. Joan impatient.*)

DECLAN Right – the cue ball was poised over the centre pocket and my ball – the striped one – was right against the top cushion and covered by about that much of his. Now, the danger was, either I'd leave him on if I missed the pot or . . . if I screwed back too much I'd . . . .

JOAN (*angrily*) You're only going on with this to annoy me, Declan, I know.

DECLAN So, I took a line on the stroke – I thought off the right cush, across the table and the gentle kiss . . . .

JOAN I only hope you're not going to continue with this when

Nuala arrives.

DECLAN   (*to Joan, testily*) And why shouldn't I? It was the greatest game of pool I ever played. What's wrong with that?

JOAN   Well, I'm not telling you again that Mr Moriarity insists that we *both* should have signed those Deeds.

DECLAN   So I chalked the cue very casually and you could hear a pin drop – even fellows at the next table came over.

JOAN   It might be only a technicality but we should both have signed it.

DECLAN   Now, I knew I had to give it plenty of side to swerve it around his solid and enough top-spin not to let it run on into the pocket . . . .

JOAN   . . . and it's not too late. We could still get those Deeds . . . .

DECLAN   So I stroked it, gently with a follow-through, perfect stroke and you could hear this gasp around the table . . . they couldn't believe what they saw . . . .

JOAN   . . . and that's what I think we ought to do . . . .

DECLAN   . . . but I could see that I'd got it exactly right . . . across the table, off the cushion and the side I'd given it brought it around . . . .

JOAN   Look, house Deeds are very important to a girl and . . . .

DECLAN   (*sudden fury*) For God's sake are you going to spend the rest of your life moaning about those bloody Deeds? What's the matter with you? Don't you trust me? Do you think I'm trying to do you out of something or what?! You'll get the bloody house whether you sign the Deeds or not!

JOAN   (*quietly*) Declan, it's just that it should be an equality. Marriage should be an equality like that. Mr Moriarity says that legally . . . .

DECLAN   Then maybe you'd better go and marry Mr Moriarity – you get on so great with him – and you can both spend the winter nights signing your bloody Deeds, *together*!

(*Silence*)

JOAN   May I have another drink please?

DECLAN   Get it yourself – if you're so mad about equality. (*pause*) Oh yeah – you're all high as kites about sharing and about equality and your rights these days – but you all become very selective very quickly. You won't buy drinks or go out and dig the roads, or open doors, or empty dustbins. Oh no – no chance of you all talking about equality there. But signing house Deeds is a different thing . . . .

(*Nuala arrives*)

NUALA   (*brightly*) Ah, hello you two.

JOAN   Ah Nuala – there you are.

NUALA   Great to get in out of that weather I can tell you.

JOAN   You're looking great.

NUALA   And you. (*to Declan*) And how is our Declan? (*No reaction. Awkward silence.*) Joan – look there's no hurry on this but I wonder would you check something out for me. Maybe you'd quietly ask Mr Moriarity for the expert opinion – Delaney is leaning on me these days, so I want the legal aspect . . . . (*Nuala realises that she is saying the wrong thing.*) Sorry – did I say something wrong?

JOAN   No no no – it's just that you've hit on the wrong subject. It's a bit too serious. The subject tonight is pool – you know, cue balls and top-spins and in-offs, you know, that kind of thing . . . .

DECLAN   (*to Joan*) What are you saying? Are you saying that I can't discuss a serious subject? Is that what you're telling her?

JOAN   (*sweetly*) Of course not, dear. It's just that pool seems to be what you like talking about tonight.

DECLAN   (*angrily, to Nuala*) Right! Then what's the subject? What's this serious subject you're investigating for your programme?

NUALA   (*shaken*) Well . . . it's not an immediate one . . . .

DECLAN   What is it about?

NUALA   Well . . . basically Housing.

DECLAN   *Basically* Housing? And what does basically Housing mean?

NUALA   Property. Ownership. Land re-zoning – you know, that sort of thing.

DECLAN   (*amused*) Land re-zoning? You're doing a programme on Land re-zoning? You? On the radio?!

NUALA   Yes.

DECLAN   (*laughs*) Oh-ho, you're on thin-ice there, missey . . . .

NUALA   I don't think it's thin-ice, Declan – I think it's a serious issue. And Joan, I do think it's about time . . . .

DECLAN   Think all you like – and while you're thinking, take my advice: don't touch it.

NUALA   I'm very sorry, Declan – but I intend not only to touch it, but to fully investigate it.

DECLAN   Do you now? Well, you could quickly regret it. I know what I'm talking about – and it's a very very serious one and not to be discussed flippantly by someone who . . . .

JOAN   There, I told you – no serious stuff to be discussed. The subject tonight is pool.

DECLAN   (*explodes*) Right! Then why don't I go and play pool and leave you two very emancipated ladies to tie yourselves up in knots talking on your very serious subjects. And by the way, if the subject should return to pool you can call the idiot back from his idiot game and he'll join in with his idiot talk!

(*Declan goes.*)

JOAN   (*pause, anxiously*) Declan?

NUALA   Ah Joan, I'm really sorry – did I say the wrong things all the way through or just . . . (*pause*) Ah, look, what's wrong Joan, what's wrong with you two?

JOAN   (*sudden anger*) Why? Why do you want to know? Do you want to do a Magazine Programme on that too?

NUALA   Joan – I only want to . . . .

JOAN   . . . Do you want to investigate us like a good, well-trained journalist? Is that the way you see everything, Nuala? Widows, Housing, Itinerants – not as a real thing that's happening to people, but material for your damn programme? Is that how they trained you? – to reduce everyone's misery to one hour of chat, and then move on to the next programme?

NUALA   Joan?

JOAN   Is everything just a radio programme Nuala? What *I*

said, what Declan said . . . . (*sobs quietly*) (*Silence.*)
(*softly*) Oh Nuala, I'm sorry. I didn't mean that. I don't
know what's happening to me.

NUALA   (*offers her a hankie*) It's okay, Joan. (*pause*) Tell me,
what is wrong?

JOAN   (*pause*) I don't know . . . . (*stops*)

NUALA   You used to get on so well . . . .

JOAN   (*pause*) It was great until recently . . . I've been going out
with him since before I left school and now . . . (*pause*) .
. . and only since we got engaged has it all begun to go
wrong. It was never like that before.

NUALA   It's probably only temporary . . . .

JOAN   Oh, if anything happened between us, I don't know what
I'd . . . (*stops*) God! What would I do if he . . . (*stops*)

NUALA   Okay . . . okay . . . okay. Would . . . would you like a
drink, Joan? (*Joan shakes her head*) Joan, if you don't
want to talk about it, well that's fine, but well all I'm
trying to say is, if you ever want to talk to anyone about
this, or anything, just call me at home or if I'm not there,
give me a ring at the station. (*pause*) Oh Joan – it's okay:
things are never as bad as . . .

JOAN   If only you knew how it feels Nuala.

NUALA   (*pause*) Yes. (*pause*) Look, let's get the drinks and take
a walk, will we? We could go out through the lounge . . . .

(*Nuala and Joan walk slowly from the pub. As they do, Alice Ryan
is in her house, listening to Radio Active. She hears Wolfman Moses
with a mixture of fear and intrigue. The music is the intro to Meat
Loaf's 'You Took The Words Right Out Of My Mouth' then:*)

W MOSES   (*howls*) Yeah, this is Wolfman Moses in his bed of blood-
red roses, on the midnight prowl and telling all you
creatures out there in the dark night to listen-out for a
little she-wolf called Nuala Ryan. (*howls*)

ALICE   Oh merciful God protect us!

W MOSES   Yeah, this she-wolf Nuala Ryan is howling and howling
on the airwaves, getting a lotta people upset and
frightened – and Wolfman Moses likes that. (*evil laugh*)
Likes people to be frightened into seeing beyond the
dark, dark darkness. So, Nuala Ryan, Wolfman Moses

listens to you and likes what you're doing – and now he
has something here specially for *you*. It's something
you'll like Nuala, from me to you – it's Dexy's Midnight
Runners. (*howls*)

ALICE   (*blesses herself*) Oh holy God – (*pause*) What's he giving
her a pair of runners for?

(*The music plays on.*)

SCENE FIFTEEN

(*Radio Active studio. It is eight o'clock. Nuala is finishing her
Magazine Programme. Justin stands around.*)

NUALA   (*at the mike*) . . . and our final letter this evening then is
from Peter O'Rourke, who says that he left school last
year after the Group Cert and has been unemployed
since that time. Peter goes on: 'nothing I learned at
school seems to be of any use when I go looking for a job,
I wonder why I had to spend all that time at school'. Well
Peter that whole subject of youth unemployment is one
we have dealt with before, but we will be returning to it
again in three weeks time, so I'm going to hold your
letter over until then. Oh and by the way I will pass on
your request for a Duran Duran record to Justin Day.
But now, with the time at one minute to eight, that's
where we must leave tonight's Magazine Programme on
the attitude of youth to education. This has been Nuala
Ryan, on the line, and I want to thank all those people
who gave their opinions, their assistance and their advice
– especially the students and teachers who took the
trouble to 'phone in. It is a subject we will return to, but
next week another Special, this time on housing, ownership and land re-zoning – and the following week our
Special will deal exclusively with women's issues. We
will have in the studio a doctor, a local Government T.D.
and a legal expert to discuss the issues of maternity
leave, stress and family planning. So questions, opinions

and views on these two Specials to me Nuala Ryan here,
on the line. But now, at exactly eight o'clock . . . .

JUSTIN Hey hey hey, it's Justin Day, your Mr Elegance saying
thanks a mill, Nuala – enjoyed every minute of your
programme and look forward to your Specials on
Housing and Women's Health. But now, it's me, Justin
Day, your Dedicated Follower of Fashion reminding
you all out there that today is still the Feast-Day of St
Melchior the Martyr, who was stoned to death. Okay
you guys, don't knock it if you haven't tried it. It's a
Justin Day Feast-Day. And I'll be taking you up to the
Wolfman Moses night prowl at ten here on . . . . (*station
jingle*)

(*Music is heard and faded as Justin takes off the cans. Nuala is
collecting her files and papers.*)

JUSTIN You . . . you going to be having many more Specials,
yeah?

NUALA Yes – oh yes. As long as the reaction is there. Tonight's
went well I thought.

JUSTIN Yeah. And there's reaction alright. Did you hear
Wolfman Moses, yeah?

NUALA No – what did he say?

JUSTIN He likes you a lot. You know he likes trouble, yeah?

NUALA Trouble! Does he? And do you listen to him at night
down there on your radio Éamonn?

JUSTIN On a radio! Don't have to listen to him on a radio, I can
hear him up here howling, laughing – and that dirty big
rat he has with him, running around here . . . .

NUALA I think that's a hamster Éamonn . . . .

JUSTIN Yeah – whatever it is – it leaves shit . . . (*stops, corrects*)
. . . it leaves excrement droppings all over the place. You
know he feeds it on Sunflower Seeds, yeah?

NUALA Yes.

JUSTIN Yeah and I have to clean it all up in the mornings after
he's kept me awake all night howling. And then he slams
the door when he's leaving. He does that just in case I've
managed to fall asleep. But you know he likes you,
yeah?

NUALA   If you say so. (*pause*) Éamonn, if no-one ever sees him, how does he get paid?

JUSTIN Paid? Delaney leaves it out for him. You never saw it, no?

NUALA   And does he stamp a card for Wolfman Moses?

JUSTIN Delaney? Stamp a card? Does he stamp a card for you, yeah?

NUALA   Yes, of course, well since I was made permanent. Does he stamp one for you?

JUSTIN Me? No, I pay Delaney for the room down there out of my wages and that's all . . . .

NUALA   So you've got no Stamp?

JUSTIN (*pause*) No.

NUALA   But that's illegal, Éamonn, you shouldn't let him do that to you.

JUSTIN (*nervously*) Hey – don't think of doing a Special on me or anything . . . .

NUALA   Well, not on *you* – but it is a subject . . . .

JUSTIN Oh no! Don't do that because they might . . . .(*looks at the turntables; to Nuala*) Hang on, don't go. (*into mike*) Culture Club there and this is your Mr Elegant, Justin Day with an advice item, sent in by 'Anxious'. Okay Anxious (*reads from a teen magazine*) You want to get rid of those unsightly spots and pimples? Okay – Justin Day advises plenty of carbolic soap and rain water and not too many of those cakes and cookies. That's it and that was another word to the wise from the Radio Active good guys, keep your questions coming in, we love to hear from you. But now let's hear from the Stones. (*plays the Rolling Stones, fades; apologetic to Nuala*) Never get anyone looking for advice really – all out of those magazines copied. You knew that, yeah?

NUALA   (*embarrassed*) No. No, I didn't.

JUSTIN You've no trouble getting letters, yeah?

NUALA   Well Éamonn – I don't have your expert knowledge of the pop world . . . nor do I know all the feast-days like you do.

JUSTIN (*pause*) Yeah, you're right. We're both experts, yeah? In our own fields. Radio Stations need experts like us, yeah?

NUALA   Yes, they do. (*looks at her watch*) Well, I'd better be going . . . .

JUSTIN   Meeting a fellow, no?

NUALA   No. I'm just going home to my mother. (*pause*) She . . . she doesn't go out much since my father died.

JUSTIN   And she expects you home on time, yeah?

NUALA   Well yes she does – so . . . .

JUSTIN   It's real vital to be on time, Nuala. Never be late. Oh, did I ever tell you about the girl I lost in London because I was late, no?

NUALA   Yes, I think so Éamonn – but I've really got to . . . .

JUSTIN   Her name was . . . . Sure – don't be late. Never be late.

(*Nuala goes. Justin pauses. Puts on the cans. Returns to the turntables. We bring up the music. Justin imitates Mick Jagger until he suddenly begins to cough convulsively. Fade.*)

SCENE SIXTEEN

(*Alice's house. Alice and Nuala. The atmosphere is tense.*)

ALICE   It's very upsetting Nuala, to be listening to the wireless and to hear the likes of that.

NUALA   Mother, I wasn't talking about the County Council – I was talking about Housing.

ALICE   And you mentioned Mr Davidson's name – your own father's colleague in the County Council.

NUALA   Did you hear what I said about Mr Davidson? I said he was the best man they had in the Housing Department but that his hands were tied with all the damn red tape and all . . . .

ALICE   God only knows what people are saying about us.

NUALA   Now Mother, this is exactly what will happen to you if you stay in this house every day – look you'll always be worrying about what people are saying. If you got out and confronted them you'll probably find that they're not talking about you at all. Go out to the choir, to Bridge, to something. Now there's something: go to the

Golden Bridge Championship on Friday-week. Well, that would be an ideal start for you.

ALICE   You needn't have dealt with the Housing at all. Surely there are plenty of other things unconnected with this family . . . .

NUALA   (*suddenly*) Mother, why do I have to come home every evening to an inquest on my programmes? You know, I too get fed-up and miserable and browned-off with the whole damn circus.

ALICE   And all those questions you were asking. Oh, your father was just like that too before we were married. Always trying to change everything, getting involved in things that didn't concern him. It's a terrible thing Nuala to be too sure of yourself.

NUALA   Too sure of myself! Mother do you really think that I'm too sure of myself?

ALICE   Well you were sure of yourself on that wireless today, asking all those questions about the Housing.

ALICE   The reason I ask all the questions is because I'm not sure. Look it doesn't mean I know all the answers – even if it sounds that way. It's just there are some things we ought to find out about, things we should know about that might need to be changed. Oh, that's all I'm trying to do.

ALICE   I know, I know – but not on your own, love. You can't be taking on the whole world single-handed you know.

NUALA   I'm not doing that – sometimes I wonder if I'm doing anything at all. But I shouldn't have shouted at you. I'm sorry.

ALICE   Look, you've just got yourself completely worn out with all of this, that's what has happened to you.

NUALA   (*quietly*) You're probably right. But Mother, why won't you go to the Golden Bridge Championship on Friday week – that'd be something – a start . . . .

ALICE   I'll tell you what I'll do – I'll think about it. (*pause, teasing*) If I don't go you won't get the Wolfman Moses fellow after me, will you?

NUALA   (*laughs*) I will – well either him or Humpy Bogart.

ALICE   Nuala, it's Humphrey!

NUALA   Oh! Congratulations

(*As they laugh together, 'Hello Stranger' by Emmylou Harris is heard to:*)

SCENE SEVENTEEN

(*At the radio station Justin Day is polishing around, Bobby Bold angrily instructing him to keep the station clean. Emmylou Harris is heard and now faded.*)

BOBBY   McGovern, will you clean up the place . . . . (*into the mike*) Thank you Emmylou and now a blast from the past, a rave from the grave, a piece of mouldy old gold that's gone from the Charts but not from our hearts – the Fab. Four – the Beatles. But before I spin it for you I've got a little competition for all you rockers out there and the prize for the first correct answer – three of Bobby Bold's Tip-for-the-Top singles. Now the question is: What was the first name of the Beatles. Their first and original name is what I want – phone in now – I'm waiting on 25145. The first name of the Beatles, 'phone in and tell Bobby Bold, rocked but not rolled. Phone in – tell me now – 25145, that's twenty-five, one-forty-five and now . . . .

(*We hear 'Love Me Do' by the Beatles for a few seconds. Then faded under.*)

JUSTIN   (*pause*) You know what the answer is, yeah?
BOBBY   Of course I know what the answer is.
JUSTIN   What?
BOBBY   (*looks at a pop magazine*) The Beatles were first called the Beat Brothers.
JUSTIN   Wrong. That was when they cut their first record. Before that John, Paul and George played skiffle and they called themselves 'The Quarrymen'.
BOBBY   Rubbish. Everybody knows they were called The Beat Brothers. Look, it's written down here.

(*The 'phone rings.*)

BOBBY   Now, we'll see. (*lifts the 'phone*) Bobby Bold, rocked but not rolled on Radio Active Quiz Time. (*pause, normal accent*) Two packets of Brillo Pads from Quinnsworth, a sliced pan and a bottle of Cod Liver Oil. Okay, love. Grand. Bye-bye. (*puts the 'phone down.*)

JUSTIN   Domestic – yeah?

BOBBY   (*reluctantly*) Yeah. (*the 'phone rings again; he lifts it enthusiastically*) Bobby Bold, rocked but not rolled on Radio Active Quiz Time. (*pause, very respectful*) I understand. (*pause*) No, no I didn't actually hear the broadcast myself – but she is a qualified journalist . . . . (*pause*) It was the News, was it? (*pause*) I agree, it's certainly not the right time to be talking about rape. (*pause*) I will indeed. And thank you for telling me about it. (*slams the 'phone down*) Did you hear the News yesterday at seven?

JUSTIN   Eh . . . no, I was cleaning up all the shit . . . .

BOBBY   She reported a rape! First thing all those kids hear on the seven o'clock News is a rape case! What the blazes is she trying to do? First she names the after hour-publicans, then she accuses property developers of bribing councillors and now rape. Next she'll be wanting to interview the bloody IRA. What the hell am I going to do . . . . (*the 'phone rings, he lifts it angrily*) Yes! What the hell do you want? (*suddenly relaxed, D.J. accent*) Oh yes – this *is* Bobby Bold, rocked but not rolled, on Radio Active Quiz Time. You got the answer to our quiz? (*pause*) Absolutely right – the Beatles were first called 'The Quarrymen'. Some folks think they were called the Beat Brothers but that was when they made their first record, right? Right – now, you've won yourself three of Bobby Bold's tip-for-the-top singles, as soon as you give me your name and address. (*pause*) Great. Thank you then, bye-bye.

(*Justin goes off, victoriously singing 'Love Me Do'. Bobby puts down the 'phone and aggressively follows him out. Bring up the Beatles 'Love Me Do' and fade.*)

SCENE EIGHTEEN

(Joan's house at downstage left. The 'phone rings and Joan answers it.)

JOAN (*into 'phone*) Hello Declan! How are you, love? (*pause*) Oh, I'm fine – but it was really hectic at the office: all wills and court cases. (*pause*) Was it? Then it's busy all around, eh? (*pause*) Oh. (*pause*) You can't get along at all? (*pause*) If you like, then, I could meet you *in* the Lounge. (*pause*)   Well, I suppose overtime is overtime. (*pause*) Yeah. (*pause*) Look, Declan – how about you coming over here to the house *after* you finish the overtime – my parents will both be at the Bridge, they're practising madly for the Competition . . . . (*stops*) I see. (*pause*) And when did you arrange this drink with the lads? (*pause*) I see. (*coldly*) Look, Declan don't you think we should have a talk sometime? (*pause*) No, not about the bloody lease. About us. (*pause, quietly*) Well, you haven't told me you loved me recently. (*pauses*) I think you could put a bit more feeling into that. (*brightly*) Hey, did you hear Nuala on last night's Magazine Special? (*pause*) Ah, Declan, that's very unfair. She was talking about Housing, not about you. (*pause*) Well, I thought it sounded very sensible. (*pause*) Yes, alright, darling – so I'll see you at the usual time tomorrow? (*pause*) Lovely. 'Bye, Declan.

(*Joan puts the 'phone down – annoyed and sad.*)

SCENE NINETEEN

(*The triangle stream of consciousness.*)

Nuala sits in the radio station, gazing silently out at us, cans on her ears. Downstage the triangle is (1) Alice in her house at downstage right – playing patience; (2) Joan in her office at downstage left – at her typewriter; (3) Declan on the building site at downstage centre – in a builder's helmet.

Each of these three will be occupied with their jobs. Throughout, on tape, we hear Nuala continually read today's news – local and international. Above this barrage of news, each of the three will suddenly speak, allowing their subconscious thoughts to surface above their jobs, in the following order:)

DECLAN (*calls*) Bring that cable across there Pat and under the roof. That's it. Grand. Onto the next house. (*quietly*) Bloody house Deeds. Well if she doesn't trust me with that, what chance can the marriage have? (*calls*) Yeah, that's grand, Pat.

ALICE (*playing cards*) Six of Spades, two of Hearts, five of Clubs. (*quietly*) Bridge Clubs. I'd like my job going up to that Bridge Club on my own. Sure, I'm grand here. Contented. God, he went so suddenly . . . . (*deals*) Ace of Hearts . . . .

JOAN (*typing, stops*) I left those letters for you to sign, Mr Moriarity. (*quietly*) If Declan would only realise that once we're married, we'd be grand. It's those lads he hangs around with, playing pool, telling him things . . . . (*types*)

ALICE If only Nuala was married itself – or going out with some nice fellow – she wouldn't be getting herself into that oul' journalism thing. That's man's work. No fellow would want a girl doing that . . . . (*deals*) Five of Diamonds . . . .

DECLAN (*quietly*) It's that Nuala Ryan – that's when it all started – when she came back. God knows what she's been telling Joan. Her and her investigations . . . .

JOAN (*stops typing*) Well if he thinks I'm going to jump every time he cancels a date, he can think again. That fellow would back out of the wedding the way he backed out of the Chris de Burgh concert. Who'd put up with that? (*types furiously*)

ALICE (*quietly*) I'd go mad in California – if I had to go. All roads and cars and sunglasses and not a body to talk to . . .

DECLAN That programme she did on Housing – ho, the nipper who makes the tea here would've done it better. What would she know anyway . . . .

JOAN Maybe Nuala is right to be out on her own, independent

like. Everyone in town knows her name – who knows
mine? Declan. Oh, but when we're married we'll be . . .
(*calls*) Oh, very well, Mr. Moriarity.

DECLAN   When you think of it, half the fellows in my class are
married already. It's the right thing to do but when . . . .
(*calls*) That's an underground connection there, Larry.

ALICE   There's Joan and Declan now – like two turtle-dove.
God knows, she knows I'm not keeping her here – sure
I'm grand here with my cards and my wireless and my
telephone. (*looks at the next card.*)

JOAN   (*stops typing*) Oh God, if he *did* leave me . . . ! I can't
even think of being without him . . . and what would I say
to everyone . . . after I going out with him since I was
seventeen . . . .

(*Blackout. All stop at once. Except Nuala's V/O Newscast continues
for eight seconds.*)

SCENE TWENTY

(*Radio station. Nuala is preparing her News, and listening to 'Day by
Day' on RTE. The station hasn't opened yet. It is 11.20 a.m. The
'phone in the station rings.*)

NUALA   (*into 'phone*) Oh, yes. Right. Okay, well that gives us an
hour then until the one o'clock News. Right. So, if the
picket is still on the factory at, say, three o'clock would
you 'phone me again and I'll give it the lead story at
three-thirty. (*pause*) Great. And thanks very much for
the info.

(*Bobby enters and Nuala puts the 'phone down.*)

NUALA   Oh, good morning, Sean.

BOBBY   (*angrily*) Don't 'good morning' me, Nuala – what the
hell is going on around here?

NUALA   Sorry?

BOBBY   Sorry? Yes, you *will* be sorry – we'll all be sorry if somebody doesn't begin to act responsibly . . . you . . . you've lost the run of yourself . . . .

NUALA   Perhaps it would be easier for me, Sean, if you told me what this was all about.

BOBBY   Sure I'll tell you: what about the programme you intend to do on Family Planning.

NUALA   I knew it! It is *not* a programme on Family Planning.

BOBBY   What is it then?

NUALA   It's a programme on Women's Health.

BOBBY   Women's Health– 'flu, chilblains, bronchitis – that sort of thing, is it?

NUALA   No, it's *not* that sort of thing.

BOBBY   Does it involve Family Planning?

NUALA   I would imagine a programme on Women's Health *would* involve Family Planning.

BOBBY   Yeah, well not *here*. You're not doing it here.

NUALA   Meaning what?

BOBBY   Meaning you can forget it!

NUALA   Forget it?

BOBBY   Yes, forget it! Put it out of your mind. Think of something else.

NUALA   But what's wrong with this, Sean? What's your reason?

BOBBY   My reason is that it's not this station's kind of programme. Now, is it twelve o'clock yet . . . ?

NUALA   Not this station's kind of . . . !

BOBBY   . . . I'll open with Leo Sayer. Where is McGovern?!

NUALA   Listen to me Sean. We've never had so much mail, so much reaction and so much advertising, this station has never been so alive . . . and purposeful . . . .

BOBBY   This is *my* station! Don't forget that! If I say that it's not this station's kind of programme, then it is not this station's kind of programme.

NUALA   What about all the mail we've received? What about our guests . . . ?

BOBBY   The TD has refused to come – and I don't blame him.

BOBBY   Because we're pirate! But the doctor has agreed . . . .

BOBBY   Oh yes – but *what* doctor . . . .

NUALA   Doctor Elaine Driscoll . . . .

BOBBY   Exactly – who's all on for distributing contraceptives out the window of her bloody motor car!

NUALA   She is a responsible and highly regarded practitioner.

BOBBY   Responsible? That's a word you shouldn't use, Nuala.

NUALA   And why not?

BOBBY   Because you don't seem to know the meaning of it!

NUALA   That's a very serious attack Sean on my professional ability to . . . .

BOBBY   Okay, okay – is it responsible to slap a rape case right in the middle of the seven o'clock News?

NUALA   Yes, it is if . . . .

BOBBY   My wife was listening to that . . . .

NUALA   Good for her.

BOBBY   And half the people in this town and county were listening and they were bloody horrified . . . .

NUALA   (*furiously*) Yes and I'm sure they'd prefer if it didn't happen, but it did and it happens a lot more than we care to admit – and it therefore matters. And bad housing also matters and the treatment of itinerants matters and rigged re-zoning matters – and women's health certainly matters and the big problem with it is that it matters to women and you are not a woman!

(*Silence. Justin – amazed comes up from his room.*)

BOBBY   (*calmly*) Look Nuala, I'll be honest about this. I'm not a great revolutionary. I don't know the ins and outs of these complex questions. I run a radio station . . . .

NUALA   Yes, exactly.

BOBBY   . . . I play music, I chat away – and it's working well, I attribute that, in no small way, to yourself. But I have a family to think about so I've got to be careful. So we steer clear of controversy for a while. We concentrate on say, doing a follow-up Special on the pollution thing . . . .

NUALA   (*shouts*) We've done that Sean . . . .

BOBBY   . . . on how it will affect the world in years to come . . . .

JUSTIN   Oh man – no one wants to hear that.

BOBBY   (*shouts*) Will you shut-up and stop sticking your dirty face in where it doesn't belong! And you get this place tidied up – right? I'm on the air now – you're all set for the News at one Nuala?

NUALA   (*calmly*) Sean, this programme has been announced for the past week, letters have already been received about it – and it's not controversial. I can promise you here and now that it will be balanced, sensible and objective . . . .

BOBBY   Like the re-zoning, I suppose?! I'll make a simple announcement cancelling it . . . .

NUALA   No, you won't, Sean. It's going out.

BOBBY   (*angrily*) It is not going out! Not in a million years is that programme going out!

NUALA   But it is all prepared and . . . .

BOBBY   I should have taken a stronger line with you a long time ago and I didn't – and what did I get?

NUALA   You got reaction, you got revenue, you got advertisers . . . .

BOBBY   I got County Councillers at my house over land re-zoning accusations, Government Deputies sending me veiled warnings about stirring-up trouble, Publicans warning me about naming names, householders threatening me about the tinkers – and I'm blowed if I am going to bring the Church down on myself on this one.

NUALA   What Church?

BOBBY   *The* Church!

NUALA   Who in the Church has said anything?

BOBBY   Doesn't matter who.

NUALA   As I thought – no one has said anything.

BOBBY   Father Peters isn't no-one!

NUALA   Father Peters? Father Peters did not object to the programme, Sean – he couldn't have! He was here on the Youth Club Programme and he loved the station. He was great. (*lifts the 'phone*) I'll talk to him.

BOBBY   (*snaps the 'phone; slams it down*) You will talk to no one!

JUSTIN   (*afraid*) Hey . . . man . . . don't . . . .

NUALA   But why?

BOBBY   The programme is cancelled, and that's that!

NUALA   But you have no reasons.

BOBBY   I don't have to have reasons – it is out!

NUALA   (*loudly*) Then so am I!

BOBBY   So are you what?

NUALA   If you kill that programme, Sean, I'm leaving.

BOBBY   You are *not* leaving! No way are you leaving!

NUALA   I am leaving! I'm finished with you and your small

minded hypocrisy! I'm finished with this whole damn place! I'm going Sean and I'm going now!

BOBBY   Then go! Go, and bloody good riddance to you too!

JUSTIN   (*shouts*) If she goes, I'm going too!

BOBBY   (*furiously*) What the hell are you talking about?

JUSTIN   (*shouts*) I said if she goes, then I . . . . (*weakens*) . . . I mean . . . I don't think . . . I wouldn't be willing to . . . I mean, if it wasn't possible for . . . Nu . . . Nuala . . . .

NUALA   (*busily packing her belongings*) Don't be silly, Éamonn – you're not involved in this.

BOBBY   (*angry but controlled*) You go, Nuala – but you'll learn. In time you'll grow-up to learn that there are things you can do and there are things you just can't do.

NUALA   I have learned, Sean! And I'm only sorry now for people like you – because you will never learn that there is a world beyond this little cocoon you think is Life and it's a world you may not like, Sean, but it's there. And it won't go away – no matter how much you try to ignore it. (*leaves angrily*)

BOBBY   (*angrily*) You're making a great mistake, young lady. A great mistake – believe you me. (*pause*) Nuala? (*pause*) Nuala?

(*Justin, afraid, turns to leave.*)

BOBBY   (*angrily*) McGovern! McGovern! You get this bloody place cleaned up. Right. And be ready to do some extra programmes until we get a replacement for that one. (*looks at his watch*) Now, what time is it – oh God I'm on the air. (*into mike, D.J. accent*) Hi, this is Bobby Bold, rocked but not rolled, welcoming you to another day here on wonderful Radio Active – the Station that cares about you. We've got music all the way opening with Leo Sayer and "I Can't Stop Loving You".

(*Bobby Bold puts on the record of "I Can't Stop Loving You". It is heard at a high speed. A pause – then Justin and Bobby rush to the turntables together to adjust it. Bobby angrily does this – glares threateningly at Justin and leaves. Justin looks after Nuala, the music is held to the end of scene and fade.*)

SCENE TWENTY-ONE

(*As music fades, the 'phone rings three times in Joan's house at DSL. Joan stands over it, nervously. Then, hopefully, she picks it up. At DSR, Alice Ryan holds her 'phone.*)

JOAN   Declan?

ALICE   Joan? This is Mrs Alice Ryan speaking.

JOAN   (*sadly*) Oh. I'm sorry, Mrs Ryan – I thought . . . I thought it was someone else.

ALICE   Joan, I was wondering if your mother was there . . . .

JOAN   No, Mammy and Daddy have both gone playing Bridge, Mrs Ryan. Tonight is the Golden Bridge Championship. It's . . . it's a very important night.

ALICE   That's what I was wondering . . . if it was tonight . . . .

JOAN   Yes. It starts at half-seven, Mrs Ryan. Are you going?

ALICE   Well – I don't know. I'll see. Thank you, Joan.

JOAN   Okay, Mrs Ryan.

(*Alice sits by the 'phone. Joan replaces the receiver, pauses and dials.*

Lights up on radio station. Justin Day at turntables playing Randy Edelman's 'Uptown Uptempo Woman'. His 'phone rings. He takes off the cans, turns down the music.)

JUSTIN   (*into 'phone*) Hey hey hey – it's Justin Day on the Radio Active Advice Spot. Hit me with your problem. Let Justin tonight make everything right!

JOAN   Oh. Oh, I was looking for Nuala – Nuala Ryan. She's on from seven to eight, isn't she? I know her. I'm Joan Moore.

JUSTIN   Hi, Joan. Joan – called after St Joan of Arc, Feast-Day the 30th of May . . . .

JOAN   Please, may I speak with Nuala?

JUSTIN   Nuala? Well, Joan of Arc, not today – today it's hey hey hey Justin Day with the helping hand slot. Problem on your mind – then lay it on me . . . .

JOAN   (*anxious*) I . . . I need to speak to Nuala . . . . personally . . . she told me I could ring her at the station if I needed . . . . Do, do you know where she is . . .

JUSTIN Negative, baby – not since yesterday when she . . . .

JOAN (*loudly*) Oh for God's sake, please – do you know where she is? I must speak with her!

JUSTIN (*pause, normal voice*) You . . . you have a real problem, yeah?

JOAN Yes, I have a real . . . please tell me where Nuala is. Please. When will she be there?

JUSTIN Here? She . . . eh . . . won't ever be . . . maybe if I give you her home number . . . her mother might . . . .

JOAN She's at home, is she? Oh, I have that number – I was on a minute ago but I thought she was at the station now. Thanks, thanks very very much – I'll 'phone her at home. (*puts the 'phone down and begins to nervously dial.*)

JUSTIN (*into 'phone*) No – I think she's gone back to Dublin . . . (*realises 'phone is dead*) I think you're . . . too late.

(*Justin turns up the sound of 'Uptown Uptempo Woman' now with the cans on, as:*

The 'phone rings in Alice's house. As it does, we see Alice Ryan take her hat and coat from the coat rack.

The 'phone continues to ring. Joan waits anxiously. Alice Ryan puts her deck of cards into her handbag, pauses to look at the 'phone, considers answering it – then decides and leaves for the Golden Bridge Championship.

The 'phone rings on – until Joan replaces it, takes off her coat and sits dejected. Immediately – a slow fade of lights on all playing areas except on Joan where lights fade slowly through the final Wolfman text. We hear this on all speakers, with echo, if possible:)

W MOSES Alright, all you wolves and she-wolves – has it been good for you tonight? It has! Well, now Wolfman Moses must abandon you for a while, so you just (*softly*) . . . turn out the light and try not to worry too much, as you . . . huddle . . . close . . . together . . . in . . . the . . . dark . . . dark . . . darkness . . . (*all lights should be gone by this*) (*a long howl*) Sweet dreams. (*laughs as Meatloaf's 'You Took The Words Right Out Of My Mouth' is heard and played to the end.*)

INTRODUCTION TO
BORDERLANDS

BORDERLANDS could only have been written for TEAM. It arose directly from the fact that the company tours the borderlands, and it emerged from our collective experience over the years which convinced us that a play which confronted "the North", and in particular young Southerners' attitudes to Northern Ireland, was necessary. BORDERLANDS, however, was not meant to be that play. Though I had been reading several British T.I.E. plays about Northern Ireland, I had approached Frank McGuinness on quite a different premise. I wrote to him first on October 13, 1983:

> *Dear Frank,*
>
> *I would like to meet you very soon to discuss the possibility of your writing a short T.I.E. play for TEAM for our Spring 1984 season. Such a script would have to be finished by October 1st 1983, and I would need to be seeing drafts in August.*
>
> *Without pre-empting our discussion, what I have in mind is a piece of 60-80 minutes duration, with a target audience of 15-17 years olds. The piece would examine language/the making of language/the uses and abuses of language/language and thought etc.*
>
> *In some way this would be a response to the dawning of Orwell's year of dread – 1984! I feel a T.I.E. piece on language is a more interesting response to this odd literary 'anniversary' than a clichéd play about Big Brother and the not so Brave New World.*

Frank McGuinness, as well as being a playwright with a considerable reputation following the success of his THE FACTORY GIRLS at the Peacock and on tour, is also a trained linguist. Indeed my earliest contact with him was at University College Dublin where he was teaching and doing postgraduate work. Born in Buncrana, close to Derry, he was familiar with Team's touring area, and I felt that for all these reasons he would be an ideal person to write TEAM's second-level play for 1984. The commission was more formal than that with Bernard Farrell. There was no period of collaboration with the actors. There was a much more direct relationship between Frank as writer and myself as Artistic Director of TEAM.

BORDERLANDS emerged from a painful process which included a very detailed scenario called GENETIVES which addressed itself to the 'given' issue of language, and a strange contemporary amorality play in seven scenes called BIGWORD. From these it was obvious that my brief about language was obstructing Frank's freedom to write. We were both unhappy but not in despair. For there was one scene in BIGWORD where we recognised the writing had emerged with strength and energy. It concerned war in a city that was clearly Derry and I remember saying to Frank that he should take this scene as inspiration and write the play from there. Having stifled him, I felt it was important simply to say to him that he should write the play he wanted to write and needed to write for an audience of young adults in TEAM's touring area. A few months later BORDERLANDS emerged with great clarity. I remember ringing Frank to tell him that he was home and dry. It had been a most difficult nine months but worth it in the end.

Ironically enough, but no doubt inevitably, BORDERLANDS *has* so much to do with language and the uses and abuses of language and that whole complex relationship between language, thought and truth which so obsessed Orwell. It is at its most obvious in the insults and graffiti and slogans of the four lads in the play, but it is there too in the anecdotes about religion and school which they exchange and which were such a forceful point of contact with young people when we toured the play. And despite my earlier reservations about Big Brother, he is definitely there in the figure of the Guard. But he is no abstraction. He is frighteningly real, not in the naturalistic sense, but rather in the direct way he gives expression to the institutional violence and the perversion of language embodied in the Criminal Justice Bill which was being debated in the Dáil while we toured BORDERLANDS, and which became central to many of the post-play workshops.

BORDERLANDS is a deliberately provocative play. We described it as a theatre parable, and indeed it has all the elements of that genre. There is a group of people from different cultures, a journey from one land to another, a temporary dwelling or tent, a central meal of bread and cider, an action of great goodness and charity and an action of great violence.

The brochure promoting the play explains further what we were attempting to achieve by presenting the play in the manner we did:

*BORDERLANDS is a theatre-parable for 1984. It shows four
young men from Derry, two Catholics and two Protestants, who
decide to bury their religious differences, and go on a charity walk.*

*We meet them on their first day across the border, as they
prepare to pitch their tent in the Republic. Although BORDER-
LANDS is about the North, there are no soldiers, no explosions,
no barricades. The four young men have come across the border
in a spirit of generosity, and address the audience directly. They
are not talking to them from inside the walls of Derry, and we
cannot think of them as being 'up there in the North'.*

*They have camped for a short while in your school, in the
borderlands of your school's consciousness and of the individual
consciences of your students. What they have to say, and what
happens to them, will challenge your students to think more deeply
about their attitudes to life and people in 'The North'.*

BORDERLANDS

by Frank McGuinness

commissioned by TEAM Theatre Company

CHARACTERS

FLUKE, a Protestant youth
LASER, a Catholic youth
ROCKY, a Catholic youth
SCOTT, a Protestant youth
VONIE, a Southern woman, in her late twenties
GUARD, ageless

SETTING
A Field

TIME
The Present

The first performance of BORDERLANDS was given in the Dominican Convent, Dun Laoire on February 8th, 1984. The play had a seven-week tour of second-level schools in TEAM's touring area. Each performance was given to a maximum of 75 students and was followed by a forty-five minute workshop. There were two performances a day in each school.

Fluke   : Lorcan Cranitch
Laser   : Brian McCollum
Rocky   : Peter FitzGerald
Scott   : Philip Hardy
Vonie   : Linda McDonnell
The Guard   : Peter Holmes

Director   : Martin Drury
Set Designer   : Bryan O'Donoghue
Costume Designer   : Nigel Boyd
Production Manager   : Vincent Dempsey
Managing Director   : Tim O'Neill

In memory of Sadie Martin, Derry woman

BORDERLANDS
A play in one act.

Fluke's hands cover his eyes.

LASER   Safe to look now.
FLUKE   Are you positive?
LASER   Would I lie to you?

Fluke uncovers his eyes and screams.

LASER   Well, what do you make of them?
FLUKE   I can't really believe it.
LASER   Do they surprise you?
FLUKE   They amaze me.
LASER   What did you expect?
FLUKE   Well, I thought they'd have at least two heads. And a holy water font at the end of each claw. Oh, and green hair, definitely green hair, with fish coming out their ears every Friday. But just look at them. They're absolutely – absolutely – revolting.
LASER   You'll have to forgive him. He's a Protestant.
FLUKE   Unionist, actually. Let's be really provocative.
LASER   First time down south.
FLUKE   In the Free State. You see, I'm not keen on zoos.
LASER   We're quite nice, us Catholics, when we're caged.
FLUKE   It upsets me though. I still think it cruel. Hi, wait a minute, Laser. Look.
LASER   What do you see?
FLUKE   One of my tribe out there.
LASER   Another Protestant?
FLUKE   Yeah. Sure of it.
LASER   How can you tell?
FLUKE   Eyes, man, look at the eyes. A dead give-away always.
LASER   Narrow?
FLUKE   Yeah.

LASER	Slanted?
FLUKE	Yeah.
LASER	Yellow skinned?
FLUKE	Yeah?
LASER	Speaks Chinese?
FLUKE	Fluent.

Fluke speaks rapid gibberish.

FLUKE	Understood every word. Agreed with it too. Inscrutable to a man. Prods.
LASER	You learn something new every day.
FLUKE	If you're as thick as you are, you do.
LASER	Since the insults have already started, could we get them over with quick?
FLUKE	Sure, Papist. You want to start?
LASER	O.K. Let's stick to the script, I'll be the Catholic, you be the Prod.
FLUKE	No, keep the customers satisfied, keep them guessing, swop. Right, go.

Rapid fire delivery

LASER	Fenian pup.
FLUKE	Orange dog.
LASER	Taig.
FLUKE	Planter.
LASER	Provo.
FLUKE	Paisleyite.
LASER	Left-footer.
FLUKE	Right-footer.
LASER	I'm getting confused. Which is which?
FLUKE	Keep it going, man. Keep it speedy. Don't think, just shout. Go!
LASER	Up the hairy mountain Down the long rope Up with King Billy To Hell with the Pope.
FLUKE	Protestant Dick went gathering sticks. Dragging his ass behind him

The ass farted Dick darted
Nobody can now find him.

LASER I haven't heard that one in years. The nostalgia of it all.

FLUKE Yeah, the joys of slagging. The names. All the names. Where are they now, the names we have lost and loved?

LASER You'll find them scrawled on the walls of Derry.

FLUKE Brits out.

LASER No Pope.

FLUKE Free Derry.

LASER Smash the hunger strike.

FLUKE We will never trade the blue skies of Ulster –

LASER For the grey clouds of an Irish Republic.

FLUKE The writing on the wall. The moving finger writes and having writ, moves on. Do you notice no romance? No John loves Mary?

LASER All passed.

FLUKE All dead.

LASER Dead.

FLUKE Don't get morbid.

LASER It has to get morbid.

FLUKE How?

LASER For a start we have to tell them why we're here. How we met and this all started.

FLUKE Not the whole thing, for God's sake.

LASER Yeah, it'll save a lot of explaining. We come from this town in the north of Ireland called Derry –

FLUKE Actually, we call it Londonderry.

LASER Dublin-derry?

FLUKE No way.

LASER Would you settle for Derryderry?

FLUKE O.K.

LASER We come from Derryderry. Now, Derryderry is divided into two parts. A Catholic side and a Protestant side.

FLUKE The Bogside and the Waterside.

LASER In the Catholic part there is a graveyard. And in the graveyard is one grave, apart from all the others.

FLUKE Getting scarey, isn't it?

LASER Shut it, Fluke. This grave stands apart from the others in this Catholic cemetery because in it lie the remains of a Protestant.

FLUKE   Sixteen years old. Killed in what is known as the fight for freedom.

LASER   Not his own side's freedom. But the other side's.

FLUKE   A traitor to the Protestants.

LASER   And a stranger to the Catholics. So he must be buried alone.

FLUKE   This would bring tears to a tombstone. But to cut a very long story short, I met this gazebo at Stephen's funeral.

LASER   I'd forgotten that, was his name Stephen?

FLUKE   What?

LASER   You called him Stephen.

FLUKE   Somebody mentioned it.

LASER   Fluke, we were the only two there. You never called him Stephen before.

FLUKE   We decided not to talk that much about it, remember? Better things to do. Getting back to essentials, I had taken my life into my hands straying that far into the Catholic jungle to reach the graveyard.

LASER   I knew what he was just by looking at him and I was determined to know why he was there.

FLUKE   But because I believe in preserving a bit of mystery, I wouldn't tell this stranger a thing. Anyway, we got talking. He asked me what was I doing that evening. Nothing, I said, I'm doing nothing. You know how it is after a funeral, bound together in grief as we were, and he was dressed very respectably and he wasn't drunk, so I couldn't really refuse to dance with him, because I'm not that kind of person, you know.

LASER   You're determined to ruin this, aren't you?

FLUKE   Yeah. Get on with the story. This is not just about us. Bring on the other two.

LASER   Rocky and Scott?

FLUKE   Aye.

Rocky and Scott enter. Rocky pushes a wheelbarrow. Scott carries a placard reading MARCHING TO DUBLIN FOR THE THIRD WORLD.

LASER   Rocky is the one pushing the wheelbarrow. Scott's carrying the placard. Rocky's a Catholic. Scott's a Protestant.

FLUKE   They adore each other. Listen.

SCOTT	Help the Third World. Collecting for the Third World. Every little helps the starving millions.
ROCKY	Our aim is a penny for every step taken from Derry.
SCOTT	Londonderry.
ROCKY	Help the Third World.
SCOTT	Hi, Rocky, can we stop soon?
ROCKY	You haven't taken your turn pushing.
SCOTT	I pushed it for two hours before getting here.
ROCKY	It's harder pushing it through a crowd.
SCOTT	How harder?
ROCKY	Everybody looks at you.
SCOTT	Isn't that what we want them to do? How can we collect money if nobody sees us?
ROCKY	Typical Prod. Thinking only of money.
SCOTT	It's not money for me, big mouth. It's for the Third World. And I don't see many Catholics refusing handouts.
ROCKY	What do you mean handouts?
LASER	Yeah, wait one minute, you.
FLUKE	PEACE.

Silence

FLUKE	Did yous all hear that? Good. Now shut up and stay shut. Rocky, Scott, come here. Now, shake hands. Shake hands, right.

Rocky and Scott shake hands, their faces daggers.

FLUKE	Good boys. Wasn't that fun? I won't let yous kiss and make up till you're engaged, I have your mothers to think of. Now, keep collecting.
ROCKY	I think we're all a bit tired, Fluke.
LASER	We've made a fair distance for the first day.
SCOTT	We're over the border.
FLUKE	Then we should get a place to camp.
SCOTT	We couldn't look for a cheap boarding house?
LASER	No, we couldn't. Aren't we supposed to be doing this for charity?
ROCKY	What has that got to do with where we stay?

LASER   Everything to do with where we stay. If we have any extra money to spend like that, it should go straight in here. (*He rattles a collecting can*) We can't expect other people to make sacrifices and not us.

FLUKE   Exactly.

LASER   So we're camping out. There's bound to be places.

ROCKY   Near the town then.

SCOTT   And with no bulls near it.

ROCKY   Definitely no bulls.

SCOTT   I'm not keen on cows either.

ROCKY   Nor me.

LASER   How do you feel about hens?

ROCKY   A hen once flew at a cousin of mine and he had a stutter for the rest of his life.

LASER   D-d-d-d-d-d-d-did he?

SCOTT   Respect the afflicted, Laser.

ROCKY   It's o.k., Scott. He was cured at Lourdes.

SCOTT   Is that a special hospital for stutterers?

ROCKY   Lourdes? No, it's a shrine to Our Lady in France. She appeared there.

SCOTT   Why?

ROCKY   Why what?

SCOTT   Why did she appear there?

ROCKY   How do I know?

SCOTT   You and Laser are Catholics. You should know.

ROCKY   She just decided to appear there. It was a miracle.

FLUKE   Does she do this appearing often? Could she show up here?

LASER   Maybe I'm just being a bit sensitive but I think that remark was a tiny bit provocative to the Catholic element in this happy ecumenical group.

FLUKE   No way. Aren't we a shining example to our divided community?

ROCKY   Burying religious differences for the sake of the starving millions.

SCOTT   Four young lads showing their troubled country the way.

LASER   God, aren't we fair great?

SCOTT   I think we're out of this world.

ROCKY   On the one road, sharing the one load.

FLUKE   Tomorrow Dublin, the next day Lourdes! What the hell

	am I saying?
LASER	Another miracle. He's converted.
SCOTT	Some chance.
ROCKY	Hi, look there.
SCOTT	Where?
ROCKY	Just ahead. That should be the perfect spot.
FLUKE	Perfect, Rocky, perfect.
ROCKY	Right, we're settled.
SCOTT	Should we ask permission?
LASER	No need. One good thing about the south is that people are friendly. I've camped here loads of times. Never once refused. I'm not trying to start a battle, honest to God, but people down here are far more open about things than we are in the north. Not always watching what they say or guarding themselves and their property. They welcome strangers.
ROCKY	We're not strangers, Laser. We're still in our own country. We don't recognise the border. We're Irish.
FLUKE	Well, we do recognise the border. Once we cross it, we're not in our own country. Whatever Irish we are, we're not your Irish. We're in the borderlands, Scott and myself.
LASER	But you're still welcome, Fluke. Don't start politics.
SCOTT	I'd be more content if we asked permission.
LASER	Permission from who? Do you want to ask the cows?
ROCKY	Cows? Come on, we're heading.
LASER	For God's sake, man, they're two fields away.
SCOTT	Why did you say to ask them?
LASER	It's just a saying country people have. Ask the cows.
FLUKE	Anyway, Laser, you think it'll be o.k. here?
LASER	Deffo. Nobody will say a dickiebird.
FLUKE, ROCKY and SCOTT:	Dickiebird, dickiebird, dickiebird.
LASER	Enough. Get the tent up, lunatics.

They start to assemble the tent. As this develops their utter incompetence at camping emerges, slowly but surely.

FLUKE	I'm looking forward to a night in the open. This is going to be great. Better than Butlins any day.
ROCKY	Never been to Butlins.

FLUKE	Is it still opened? I thought they closed it down when the Northerners stopped going.
SCOTT	Why did they stop going?
FLUKE	The bother. The troubles. The civil rights disturbances. Remember those good old days, Rocky? Before them, mostly Belfast ones went down to Butlins. They wouldn't travel south now. I suppose they think they wouldn't feel welcome, even in a holiday camp.
ROCKY	What do they want as a welcome? Bonfires at the border?
SCOTT	There were enough fires burning in Belfast.
ROCKY	Who started the burning?
SCOTT	Do you want three guesses?
ROCKY	If you're referring to the Belfast Catholics, mate, I'll have you know that I look on them as heroes. When the Derry Catholics were defending themselves from your mob, the Belfast ones, against all the odds, gave them support to carry –
SCOTT	If you call tearing the heart out of a place support –

Fluke rapidly intervenes to separate Scott and Rocky.

FLUKE	I know nothing about tents, Laser. Where's this to go?
LASER	I'm not sure. Just leave it there. And get on with the job in hand, yous two.
ROCKY	I thought you said you'd camped out loads of times?
LASER	I have.
SCOTT	Then how come you don't know where everything goes?
LASER	Give me a chance. I need a bit of time. I've only two hands.
FLUKE	You should have some idea where –
LASER	Look, don't rush me, Fluke. I'll manage it. I hate being rushed. Wait. I'll get it up in my own sweet time. Keep your traps shut. Do as you're bid. That way you help me. O.K.?

Silence

LASER	I said O.K.?
FLUKE	O.K. by me, if you know what you're doing.

LASER	I know what I'm doing. All right?
SCOTT	Let's see you doing it then.
LASER	Right. Right, Fluke. Don't move from there. That's your corner. Keep to it. That's your responsibility. Hold on to what you have and don't let go.
FLUKE	Right you be.
SCOTT	What about this?
LASER	The string? Pull it. Stretch it a bit. Take it easy though. Don't force it. Try too hard and it will all collapse. You have to be gentle.
SCOTT	Right, sorry, Laser.
LASER	You exactly the same, Rocky.
ROCKY	Nice and easy?
LASER	That's the way.
FLUKE	Everybody's got their corner?
LASER	Just stick together and it will stand.
SCOTT	Can I let go of it, Laser?
LASER	Have more patience, wait till I tell you.
FLUKE	Laser, are you sure we'll all fit into this? It's a bit wee.
LASER	We can all squeeze in. If there's not enough room, we'll make enough.
FLUKE	One of us might have to stay out.
LASER	Not if we watch. It's not a hotel you're in. It's home for the night. We can rough it a bit.
FLUKE	We'll be sleeping on top of each other.
ROCKY	Oh goodie, bags I Scott.
SCOTT	Do you want your mouth broken?
LASER	Don't move.
SCOTT	Did you hear what he said?
FLUKE	Only a joke.
SCOTT	Some joke.
ROCKY	Oh Scott, and you promised you'd be nice.
SCOTT	I'm warning you.
LASER	Give it a rest. Stay where you are. Yes, very nice piece of work. Well done, though I say it myself.
FLUKE	Laser, maybe I'm thick or something, but I thought we might be spending some time inside the tent.
LASER	That's the general idea of having a tent.
FLUKE	Then if we're holding it up outside, how can we get inside?

LASER   Who says you're holding it up?

They each let go of their respective ends. The tent collapses. Rocky and Fluke laugh.

SCOTT   I don't think it's funny, Laser.

LASER   I'm not exactly splitting my sides either, Scott.

FLUKE   How many times have you camped out, mate?

LASER   loads of times.

ROCKY   How many is loads of times?

LASER   About a dozen.

FLUKE   How many's in a dozen?

LASER   Everybody knows –

FLUKE   How many's in your dozen?

LASER   Three.

FLUKE   Did you put up the tent?

LASER   Well, the brothers were there. I gave a hand.

FLUKE   What kind of hand?

LASER   Well, I watched them. I thought it was easy.

FLUKE   Did you? Now watch me doing it.

LASER   I tried it at home last night. They were teaching me. We were doing more or less the same thing as I was getting you to do. I don't know what's wrong. Maybe it works differently outside.

FLUKE   No, it works differently when you cross the border. Another country. Alien territory. Different vibrations. Never fear. We shall overcome. Protestant craftsmanship here. Catholic enthusiasm there. Unbeatable combo when they work together. Watch this. This contraption will go up and stay up. Figure it out. Put this pole, say here, and measure the length of the roof, which is minus, say the – hold on.

Fluke finds the bag of tent pegs.

FLUKE   Eureka!

ROCKY   What's that for?

FLUKE   I haven't a notion.

SCOTT   You're a big help.

FLUKE   Of course. pegs! We're not putting it up in the kitchen now, Mucker. Come on.

They start to reassemble the tent. As they work, Fluke starts to hum 'Have you heard about the big strong man?' The others join in.

LASER   I think we're getting somewhere.

SCOTT   Thank God. I just want a place to kip.

ROCKY   This is definitely getting better.

FLUKE   Yeah, I think it's holding this time.

LASER   Make sure of that. Don't let it fall.

SCOTT   Look who's talking.

LASER   I did my best.

FLUKE   You did indeed. You always do.

LASER   I think I've had enough stick. Lay off.

FLUKE   I mean it. Here we are. Our own nook. A small spot we can call our own for this evening anyway, right?

ROCKY   Is anybody hungry?

SCOTT   See me? See that tent? I could eat it.

FLUKE   Don't, Scott. Leave it for the cows in the middle of the night.

SCOTT   Shut it.

FLUKE   Mooooooo.

LASER   You were right, Fluke. The tent. It is pretty small for four. We usually sleep three in it. Made a balls-up again.

SCOTT   What will we do then?

FLUKE   We'll manage. We have to. Share the space. Whatever's there, share it. My old fella's philosophy.

SCOTT   Your old fella's a Communist.

FLUKE   A Communist? He calls himself a staunch supporter of the international labour movement. It's his one little luxury in the present recession. He's a bit worried that his remaining son and heir hasn't had a chance yet to share the burden of the great working class, but I still think there's a lot in this sharing, especially where grub's concerned. Remember the Third World? (*He raises a collecting can*) Well, it's here. It's me. I'm hungry. Feed me. Who's got the goodies?

ROCKY   Me.

LASER   Will we have a fry-up? I can get the wee stove going. That's my job when we're out. I can do that definitely.

ROCKY   The ma packed me some things.

LASER   Sausages and bacon and stuff?

ROCKY   No, sandwiches and things. There's loads.

FLUKE   Get them. If we're still hungry, we can fry up afterwards.

LASER   Come on, Rocky. We'll fill a can of water from the stream.

Laser gets a can from his rucksack.

ROCKY   Can't you go yourself for a can of water?

LASER   No, I can't. I'm scared of cows as well.

ROCKY   Hypocrite. Come on.

Rocky and Laser exit.

FLUKE   O.K., sunshine?

SCOTT   Why should I not be?

FLUKE   Why indeed? Only asking.

SCOTT   Funny looking country this, isn't it?

FLUKE   How funny?

SCOTT   Really green, you know.

FLUKE   Is it? I must be colour-blind. I think it's red.

SCOTT   How red?

FLUKE   Maybe . . . maybe it's the cows.

SCOTT   You're smart, aren't you?

FLUKE   Very. Never lost for words. Then, neither are you.

SCOTT   What do you mean? I can't string two words together. If I could, who'd listen to me? I even find myself boring.

Fluke snores.

SCOTT   You don't know what it's like, Fluke. Look at you. You're at your ease already with those two.

FLUKE   Why are you not?

SCOTT   Rocky strikes me at times as dangerous. You heard him giving out about Belfast. Hot-headed stuff.

FLUKE   I heard you as well, hot-head.

SCOTT   He started it.

FLUKE   You were willing to finish it.

SCOTT   You have to stick up for your own side sometimes.

FLUKE Who are your own, Scott? I always though you believed
       you were just a bore, all on your own.
SCOTT Do you believe that?
FLUKE I think . . . I think you're out on your own. A case apart.
SCOTT Shut up.

Silence

SCOTT I know down here who my own are. No matter how those
       two Taigs may look at me, I'm going to church here this
       Sunday.
FLUKE Count me out of that, kiddo.
SCOTT You're going whether I have to haul you. I hope we can
       find a church.
FLUKE I'd say you'd have no bother. A whole variety pack to
       choose from. Take your pick. Quaker oats? Rice Krispie
       Roman Catholic? Frostie Free Presbyterian? Branbud
       Baptist? All the one. All guaranteed to have the same
       effect. Give you the runs away from reality.
SCOTT Don't blaspheme, Fluke.
FLUKE Why not.
SCOTT You mock God at your peril.
FLUKE He's mocked us enough. I'll chance his sense of humour.
SCOTT Look, I told the ma I'd go.
FLUKE She's not my ma.
SCOTT I told her I'd make you go.
FLUKE I'm not going.
SCOTT I promised.

Fluke lifts one finger.

FLUKE That's my promise.
SCOTT I see them coming back. Control your tongue. We can't
       let the side down?
FLUKE Whose side? What side?
SCOTT Answer that yourself. Yours is the one family that
       should know about sides.
FLUKE I warned you to say nothing about –
SCOTT It just come out. I didn't forget. O.K. Take it easy.
FLUKE No, you take it easy, son. I'm not here to fight the Battle

of the Boyne. We have to share a tent with those two. Take a look at the tent, Scott. Walk about it. Look inside. Small, isn't it? Too small to have sides and keep to them. There's just no room for fighting.

SCOTT   Maybe not, but I have a secret weapon.

FLUKE   What?

SCOTT   My feet smell.

Rocky and Laser enter.

ROCKY   We're back. I'm starved. Good job the ma packed enough sandwiches to feed a regiment.

From his rucksack Rocky produces a gigantic bag of sandwiches.

FLUKE   What regiment was she in training for? Feeding the Falklanders?

ROCKY   Forget the Fucklanders. We'll make short work of them. I have ham, tomato, cheese, egg and onion.

SCOTT   Ham and tomato disagree with me. Give us egg and onion.

ROCKY   The rest of you help yourself. I suppose nobody else wants a black pudding sandwich. I'm mad about them.

FLUKE   Black pudding sandwiches?

ROCKY   Delicious. Especially with a fried egg in the middle. They're that thick with stuff the egg dribbles down your chin and you can suck it up like this.

Rocky slurps.

SCOTT   I've just gone off egg and onion as well.

LASER   Listen, I better light the stove.

FLUKE   For what?

LASER   Tea. The throat's cut off me. I need something to wet it.

FLUKE   Hold it. Say no more. Get your mugs.

They get a mug from their rucksacks. Fluke produces a carton of cider.

FLUKE   La-da! La pièce de résistance, gents!

LASER	Why did you bring that, Fluke?
FLUKE	What do you mean why did I bring that?
LASER	If you had money to throw around you on boozer, you could have been better put to give it to a good cause.
FLUKE	This is for us. We're a good cause.
LASER	There are better ones.
FLUKE	Are there, Laser? Tell me about them.
LASER	You know all about them.
FLUKE	The beloved starving millions?
LASER	If you feel like that, why are you on this march?
FLUKE	You're so sure of yourself you tell me.
LASER	I don't understand why you –
FLUKE	No, I have a feeling you don't understand, which is surprising. I'm on this march because for once I thought it might be possible to do something like this without being surrounded by pains-in-the-arse forever telling me what to think. Maybe I was wrong.
LASER	Is that what you think of me? A pain-in-the-arse?
FLUKE	Answer that yourself.
LASER	Well, I'm very sorry to have let you down.
FLUKE	You have.

Fluke pours himself a drink from the carton and holds out his mug.

FLUKE	Cheers.

Laser grabs the mug, looks at Fluke, looks at the drink, raises the mug high above Fluke's head, retracts suddenly and downs the cider in one.

LASER	O.K.?
FLUKE	Sorry.
LASER	So am I.
FLUKE	My mistake.
LASER	Mine too. How about a refill?
FLUKE	Go ahead. Rocky?
ROCKY	Sure. Why not?
FLUKE	Scott?
SCOTT	I don't drink.
FLUKE	This is called cider, Scott. It's not alcoholic.

SCOTT   Is it not? I may as well.

FLUKE   Hypocrite.

SCOTT   Is it alcoholic?

FLUKE   You know it is.

SCOTT   You won't tell the ma?

FLUKE   Dickiebird.

ROCKY   Anybody want more sandwiches?

SCOTT   Throw us one.

ROCKY   Cheese this time?

FLUKE   Give him tomato.

SCOTT   I told you tomatoes don't agree with me.

FLUKE   You know what to do when things don't agree with you? Answer them back, Scott. Fight them. If you can't beat a tomato, you'll not beat much else.

SCOTT   The ma never gives them to me.

FLUKE   Defy her.

SCOTT   You could have a sick man on your hands, Fluke.

FLUKE   Correction, he'll be on your hands, Scott. And on your sleeping bag.

ROCKY   Well, do you want a tomato sandwich?

SCOTT   Give us one. In for a penny, in for a pound. I'm no pansy.

FLUKE   True enough, even if you do wear underpants with flowers on them.

ROCKY   What?

SCOTT   For God's sake.

FLUKE   Lovely wee flowers.

SCOTT   The ma bought them.

LASER   Aaah! Scott's ma strikes again.

SCOTT   They were going cheap at a sale. You know women. They'd put a man into anything. Couldn't watch them. I mean, have you ever forgiven your mother for christening you Laser?

LASER   For God's sake that's not my real name. It's a nickname.

SCOTT   Why Laser?

ROCKY   Because he's a wee ray of light.

LASER   Give it a rest.

ROCKY   No, he got the name at school. Wasn't it the primary?

LASER   Don't remember.

ROCKY   I do now. It was the last year of primary. The teacher called you it.

LASER   She was a sarcastic wagon.

ROCKY   She meant it. Laser always settled the fights in the playground. Well, he tried to. He got more knocks than the
ones fighting. I once got you in the nose, remember?

LASER   I got you back, and you know where, remember that?

ROCKY   A true peacemaker.

FLUKE   A living saint.

LASER   No way, mate. Not a saint.

ROCKY   That's true. The heathen caused uproar when he
stopped attending religion classes.

LASER   They had nothing to do with religion.

ROCKY   Listen, you can carry the ecumenical thing too far.

LASER   Maybe it's time somebody did carry it too far.

SCOTT   How do you mean?

LASER   How come it took me all these years to meet you and
Fluke? Two ordinary blokes I like and can talk to?

SCOTT   You don't know me. How can you like me?

LASER   I'd still like to look on you as my mate. But I'm expected
to look on you as my enemy. My inferior.

SCOTT   I'm no inferior.

LASER   Who said you were.

SCOTT   You did.

LASER   No, my religion did. In the same way your religion
taught you to look on me and Rocky here as an inferior.
What kind of religion divides people the way we've been
divided? What kind of religion sets people at each
other's throats, or breeds hate in the name of its God?
Who is he anyway? Do we know? Do the ones teaching
us know? I doubt it. They're not even sure what to call
knowing him. In primary school it was catechism. Then
it turned into religious education. That changed one year
to religious knowledge. And when I'd had enough of
that, hey presto, it was termed christian doctrine. What
did they call religion in Protestant schools?

FLUKE   History.

LASER   You see what I'm getting at. After a dose of their Christian doctrine we stoned each other coming home from
school. They're a shower of hypocrites, and so are we if
we believe them.

SCOTT   That's not fair, Laser.

ROCKY Scott's right there. You can't get away with sweeping statements like that.

SCOTT There's good and bad on all sides, Catholic and Protestant.

LASER And what I say is that in the north, good and bad don't come into it. Only us and them. Fenians and Orangemen. Take your partner and hate the other side. Love your neighbour? Do you realize what that would mean at home if we actually try to do it? But we won't, because we're scared. We're afraid to know them, let alone love them. And that fear will be the end of us.

Fluke applauds slowly and mockingly.

FLUKE He is called Laser because he burns clean and bright and because he sees things so clearly that he might even blind himself to being wrong, very wrong. So he better be careful in case he burns himself out.

LASER Is that the best you can answer? How am I wrong?

FLUKE Because you're still attending religion classes, Laser. Get out of the church onto the streets, sir, start looking for work. Your fellow Christians aren't in command any more. Your big firms, they're the saviours of your country, north and south, boy. What they say goes. (*Fluke bows*) Good morning, Mr. Courtauld. (*Fluke salutes*) Nice to see you, Mr. Dunlop. (*Fluke waves*) And goodbye to you, poor wee Mr. de Lorean. You're out of date, Laser. It's still, yes, boss, no, boss, three bags full, boss, except now it's multinational boss. That's a big word, children, isn't it? Multinational. Let's hear you all say it. MUL-TI-NAT-ION-AL. Very good. That big word's the master now. We're all natives to it, children, all inferior, Fenians and Orangemen alike. Why is that so? Well, you see, they have the work. We beg them for work. They give it out. And in return we give ourselves, until they no longer want us, and we're dumped. When you're dumped, it makes no difference standing in a dole queue whether you're a Fenian or an Orangeman.

ROCKY The big difference being that there are a damned sight more Fenians than Orangemen in the dole queue.

FLUKE Well if Fenians take enough consolation from that to do nothing but blame the Orangemen and let blame stop there, then they deserve to be in the dole queue. They're playing into the master's hands. Oh good man, Rocky. Stand up for your own. But who is your own? We'll fight that out among ourselves and we'll be so busy fighting we won't have time to fight the new masters. And they're a damned sight bigger than the Brits. That concludes the history lesson. And the religious among you can take it as Gospel. For it's what my daddy says. And I believe him. Because my daddy is great. Poor. Inferior. Protestant. But fair great. You wanted an answer, Laser. You've got it. Cheers.

SCOTT When your da gets going, do you know who he reminds me of? Ian Paisley.

ROCKY That's your cover blown, Fluke.

SCOTT I mean it as a compliment, full of passion, you know.

FLUKE Thanks, I'll tell him you said that, he'll be over the moon.

LASER Rocky, can I have more cider?

ROCKY Yeah.

SCOTT I take it Rocky's a nickname as well?

ROCKY Yeah. From the film, ROCKY. I fancied myself as a bit of a boxer. Didn't come to much. Trained for a good while, I enjoyed that. But I was no good in the ring.

SCOTT Had you many bouts?

ROCKY Only five. Knocked out in every one of them. First round every time, except the last. That was a real disgrace.

SCOTT Why a real disgrace if you finally made round two?

ROCKY It was pretty embarrassing. I was boxing my sister.

SCOTT Who?

ROCKY The sister. She's a pretty sharp wee fighter. She's kept the game on. They call her Rocky 2.

SCOTT Rocky, give up boxing.

ROCKY Oh I have. But I'm thinking of wrestling next. I'm trying to find a name at the minute. A name's important in the ring, especially if it's funny. It can drag in the crowds. Fluke would be a good wrestling name. Yeah, I like it. Is there a Protestant saint called Fluke?

FLUKE Me. I canonised myself.

SCOTT   That's right. I don't remember anyone giving you that name.

ROCKY   Why Fluke?

FLUKE   Because I'm the exception that proves the rule. The one in a million that makes it all seem possible. For despite all the evidence, I remain optimistic about our future. (*mockingly*) Yes, I'm foolish enough to believe that better times are coming to Ulster. The churches, once so divisive, now pray together for reconciliation. Mostly at funerals. And young people are increasingly rejecting violence for brotherhood.

Laser begins to whine.

FLUKE   I know this may not be easy to accept.

Laser growls.

FLUKE   What kind of religion divides us from each other?

Laser snaps at Fluke's ankles. Fluke wards him off.

FLUKE   What kind of religion sets people at each other's throats?

Laser goes for Fluke's throat.

FLUKE   I surrender. I surrender.

ROCKY   You've got it wrong, Fluke. It's No surrender. No surrender.

FLUKE   The air of the south is affecting me badly.

LASER   Oh no, remember, you will never trade the blue skies of your Ulster for the grey clouds of an Irish Republic?

ROCKY   Right?

LASER   (*sings*) On the green grassy slopes of the Boyne

ROCKY   (*sings*) Where we fought for our glorious religion,
              Where? On the green grassy slopes of the Boyne.

FLUKE   and SCOTT It was worn at Derry, Aughrim,
              Enniskillen and the Boyne.
              My father wore it as a youth
              in bygone days of yore.

ALL   And on the twelfth I love to wear

The sash my father wore.

SCOTT That was lovely. Do you come here often?

FLUKE The south? Only when the Pope's visiting.

SCOTT He's lovely, isn't he?

FLUKE A darlin' man, a darlin' man.

All four continue celebrating. Vonie enters, unnoticed.

VONIE Who the hell do you think you are?

SCOTT What?

VONIE What are you doing here?

FLUKE Dancing in the borderlands.

VONIE Don't give me cheek. This is private property. I want you out of this field in five minutes flat.

SCOTT What harm are we doing?

VONIE Five minutes I said, do you understand English? If you don't go, I'll call the guards to make you go.

LASER We asked what harm are we doing here?

VONIE This is not a camping site. If you want one, find it. I'm not providing it.

FLUKE We're not asking you to provide anything. We just want to stay for the night.

LASER We're marching, you see –

VONIE I want to know nothing about your march. I'm not interested in politics. All I want you to do is march out of this field, my field.

LASER It's not politics. We're collecting –

VONIE I know all about collections of your type. We're not completely stupid down here. Now, just gather your belongings and clear out.

LASER If you'd only listen for a –

VONIE No, you listen to me. I'm sick and tired listening to your like whinging and whining whenever I switch on the television. I'm fed up hearing what you're going through. I'm sick of checkpoints and helicopters and army jeeps. It's been going on too long up there. One time you might have had my sympathy, but not anymore. Whatever you've got you've brought on yourselves. We've had enough of you. We're tired listening. We're tired of it all.

FLUKE   Join the club, lady.

ROCKY   Look, listen –

VONIE   I want you out of –

SCOTT   Why should we listen to you if you won't give us a hearing?

VONIE   I've heard enough. If I can't move you, the guards will. They know your type.

FLUKE   What type is that?

VONIE   Parasites.

Laser rapidly shakes a collecting can.

LASER   Help the parasites. Save them. Hear them.

VONIE   Don't threaten me. It'll only make things worse for you. I'm warning you.

FLUKE   Get your guards, woman.

Silence

FLUKE   Go on.

VONIE   I'm afraid to.

FLUKE   Why?

VONIE   I'm afraid to turn my back while he's holding that.

Laser drops the can. Money rolls everywhere. Vonie exits.

FLUKE   Well, Laser? I'm not trying to start a battle, but are people in the south more open and generous? Not always watching themselves or their property. They welcome strangers, eh? We're not strangers, right, Rocky. We're in our own country. Wrong. We're not. None of us are.

SCOTT   I said we should have asked permission.

ROCKY   I hate the police being called in. It's not worth the hassle. We should move quick.

LASER   No. No, we'll wait and see.

FLUKE   Good. My sentiments exactly. Sit tight. I wouldn't miss this for the world. Would you? Pity though. It happened just when we were getting started. Who cares? Where were we? Ah yes. Doing our tribal dance. Forgetting

ancient differences. Differences so old they've turned
into similarities despite ourselves. Wasn't that it, Laser?

LASER   Something like that.

FLUKE   Foolish, very foolish. Sad, very sad. Ah dear me. When
you grow as old as Laser and me, young fellas, you find
things get sadder all the time.

ROCKY   Thanks, granda.

SCOTT   I don't know about that. Some things get better. When I
was a kid the saddest thing in my life was that nobody
gave me a nickname. Just to show I was different enough
to be important. I even gave myself one but they never
caught on. Now I'm glad I never had any name but my
own.

ROCKY   Why?

SCOTT   I'm called after my father. Scott was his name.

ROCKY   He's dead?

SCOTT   Yeah.

ROCKY   Recent?

SCOTT   No, no. A good few years ago. Just at the bother's
height.

ROCKY   In the bother?

SCOTT   Yeah.

ROCKY   What happened? Was he shot?

LASER   Give it a rest, Rocky.

SCOTT   No, it's all right, Laser. I'm well over it. I can talk about
it. No, he wasn't shot. No. A bomb. Under his car.
Blown to bits. Outside the house. He was an RUC man,
Rocky. On his way to work. Funny enough, well it's not
funny, he was giving a neighbour a lift to work as well.
He did it every day. She was a Cathlic. Really nice.
Nobody knew if it was her or my da they were getting at.
Her man never got over it. My mother did. She's great,
you know the ma, Fluke. No bitterness. She wouldn't let
us be. Not bitter at all. Don't hate Catholics. I mean, one
died with my da. I don't hate them, do I, Fluke?

FLUKE   No.

SCOTT   When Fluke told me, Laser, about this mate of his that
was making this march, and that it was to Dublin and
that he was a Catholic, I was the only one in our crowd
who didn't tell him to piss off, because it's a good cause,

the Third World. Think we've got problems. God, see them people on TV. Cut the heart out of you. We're blessed compared to them. So I said I'd go. Bit of crack on the way, maybe, as well. Which we've had, and I'm enjoying myself. Well, I was until that wagon arrived. But the main thing is I'm not bitter against you, am I?

ROCKY   No way.

LASER   Do you think you should be bitter?

SCOTT   What point, Laser? Doesn't everybody have somebody belonging to them or at least know somebody destroyed by the bother?

ROCKY   We have ones belonging to us in Long Kesh.

SCOTT   What are they in for?

ROCKY   Nothing, Scott. They were all framed. No court in any other country would have put them away. They were treated like dogs. And they're innocent. Completely innocent. It'll be proved someday. My ma sounds like yours. She says if you pray hard enough, then God's good and he'll find a way out, if you make enough sacrifices. She wanted me to go on this march. Between her and Laser's forcing I had no choice.

SCOTT   Yes.

ROCKY   Who claimed your father's bombing?

SCOTT   What odds?

ROCKY   Just asking.

SCOTT   Nobody did as a matter of fact.

ROCKY   Then it couldn't have been the Provos.

SCOTT   Why the hell not?

ROCKY   When they do something, they claim it. Say what you like against them, but they're man enough –

SCOTT   Man enough. You call what was done to my father the actions of a man. What kind of man would –

ROCKY   Do you call what's done to people in your Majesty's prisons the actions of men? Let me put you wise to what your da's pals in the RUC get up to with their big batons and their fists and their wee electric shocks. That's if you can bear to hear the truth.

SCOTT   Don't bother. I have a growing suspicion that maybe your ones aren't so completely innocent, Rocky.

ROCKY   And I have a growing suspicion that maybe you're a lot more bitter than you let on, Scott.

SCOTT My father was murdered.

ROCKY Maybe he deserved it.

LASER Oh God.

SCOTT Your type are all the same. You really are.

ROCKY So are yours, friend. So are yours.

Laser separates them, seeing the guard.

LASER That's enough. Here comes more trouble.

Vonie and Guard enter.

GUARD These are the gentlemen in question?

VONIE Yes.

GUARD Were you told to leave?

Silence

GUARD I said were you not told to leave?

FLUKE I suppose we were.

GUARD You suppose, son? You don't suppose in these parts. You do as you're told. Move. I see you've been enjoying yourselves. That's good. The party's over. Where did you pick up the cider?

FLUKE Home.

GUARD Where would home be? Across the border?

SCOTT Aye, thank God.

GUARD Just mosey on back across the border. We don't need your custom.

LASER We can't.

GUARD Can't?

LASER We're on our way to Dublin.

GUARD What would be your business in Dublin?

ROCKY We're pushing this wheelbarrow from home to Dublin. We're collecting enough coins to fill the barrow.

SCOTT It's for charity.

LASER The Third World.

GUARD Third World? Charity? Cider, more like, eh?

FLUKE We've money of our own for that.

Guard points at spilt money.

GUARD   But this is the way you thank people stupid enough to believe that story? Throwing their money away? Maybe you just pocket most of it.

ROCKY   We pocket no money. We've nothing to hide.

GUARD   We all have something to hide. Where would people like me be if we didn't?

LASER   Why don't you just leave us alone?

GUARD   So you shower can march in here where you're not wanted? No way, boyo. You're trespassing where you don't belong. You've broken the law. I'm here to keep it.

SCOTT   If we had known –

GUARD   If you had known? You should have known. Should have known respect for the privacy of what's not yours. Ah maybe we're being too hard. Where you're from there's not much respect for anything, is there? Life or limb. The law of the jungle. That's all these boys understand. But it's different here. This country's civilised. No packs of savages blowing the brains out of each other. But don't think we're soft. If all you know is the rule of the fist, if that's what keeps you in order, we won't be scared to use it. Isn't that right?

VONIE   I'm not sure I like what you're about.

GUARD   Maybe not, but you'll still depend on me to do it.

VONIE   How do you mean depend?

GUARD   Who was the one who asked me to come here? Anyway, I'm not finished yet. Let's see what they're carrying?

Guard lifts one of the rucksacks.

GUARD   Whose is this?

Silence

GUARD   Come on.

SCOTT   Mine.

Guard opens and searches the rucksack, finally discovering a pair of floral underpants.

GUARD   So this is what the hard men wear? Who bought you these? The boyfriend?

ROCKY   Get your hands off his belongings.

GUARD   Are you worried in case –

ROCKY   I said leave his stuff alone.

GUARD   Or else? Let's see what the rest of you are hiding.

Guard reaches for another rucksack. Rocky tries to grab it from him. Guard swipes at Rocky and floors him.

VONIE   For God's sake, stop this.

GUARD   Get him up.

VONIE   What's got into you? They're no more than youngsters.

GUARD   They're youngsters now, are they? You didn't think that when you came running to me, panicking that you wanted them off your land.

VONIE   They can be got rid of without you lifting your big fist. Are you all right, son?

Vonie goes to Rocky.

GUARD   Can they? I doubt it. You shift this type by one means only. When you order them out, you make sure they go.

Guard starts to dismantle the tent.

GUARD   Just clear them out. Hear no excuses. That's where the Brits made their first mistake. Giving them any sympathy. We won't make that mistake. They won't walk on us when they travel down here. That should prepare them for the day when they get their big wish. Are you all wee Provies, lads? Don't be. They don't look very far forward. They might be able to give us a hard time now. But they'll get a harder time when we have full rein in their united Ireland. They might regret wanting that.

FLUKE   Will they get their united Ireland?

GUARD   Will we get it? I think so.

LASER   Will you be let away with as much in it?

GUARD   What do I get away with? As much as your RUC get away with. And do you know why? The silent majority is right behind us. Isn't that so, woman?

VONIE   Get off my land.

GUARD   Your land? You may own it, but I guard it. What's the difference?

VONIE   A big difference. A very big one. And as long as I'm here it'll stay a big difference. Leave now.

GUARD   Or what will happen?

VONIE   We still have ones over you in this country. Ones you have to answer to. You can be reported.

GUARD   To who? The ones over me? Go ahead with your report. Bring our northern guests back to act as witnesses. That's if they'll recognise the court. But take my advice, lads. Clear out. Stop collecting for the Third World. You need a licence to collect money here. I don't imagine you bothered to find that out.

Guard moves to exit, then looks back.

GUARD   Anyway, where's this Third World?

FLUKE   You're living in it.

GUARD   Am I? Surely not. That's your country. Get back to your Third World up there. It's where you belong. Who else wants you?

Guard exits.

FLUKE   Get the stuff together.

LASER   Right.

SCOTT   Come on, Rocky, are you fit to stand?

ROCKY   Aye.

SCOTT   Knocked out in round one again, sir.

ROCKY   Why spoil a perfect record?

They collect their belongings.

FLUKE   Are you waiting for something?

VONIE   I'm sorry. I never thought he would react like that. He's not the usual type. The ones I know, and I know some well, are decent. From him, you wouldn't think that.

They ignore Vonie.

VONIE   There's no need to leave. I lost my head earlier. I have two kids. They spent their time today roaring. I flew off the handle when I saw you in the field. You know yourself, with young ones, you can't be too careful with strangers.

FLUKE   At any age you can't be too careful with strangers.

VONIE   Please, you can stay. I really respect what you're doing. If I'd known earlier –

LASER   We tried to tell you.

VONIE   But if I'd known, I would have avoided all this. We do a lot of sponsored walks in this parish. Fasts at Christmas. I try to support them all. I try – oh God, I'm sorry he went for you like that. Are you all right?

ROCKY   It's all right.

VONIE   I will report him definitely.

ROCKY   What point?

VONIE   I'm really –

LASER   Sorry. We know.

VONIE   I'm asking you to stay.

FLUKE   No.

VONIE   You're welcome.

FLUKE   It's too late.

VONIE   I can't force you.

FLUKE   No, you can't.

Vonie offers Rocky hand.

VONIE   I'm Vonie.

ROCKY   I'm Rocky.

They shake hands. Then she shakes hands with Scott and Laser, exchanging names. Fluke refuses her handshake.

FLUKE   Go home to your house. Go home to your small children. Go home to your private property. Enjoy it.

	It's all yours.
VONIE	It is. Not much, but it is mine. Do you begrudge me that?
FLUKE	I begrudge you what I think of you. Nothing.
VONIE	You might learn to think differently.
FLUKE	So might you.
VONIE	I'm willing to hear why I should.

Silence

VONIE	Can I say more than that?

Silence

VONIE	Do I not desedrve an answer? I've just tried to protect you.
FLUKE	You were protecting yourself.
VONIE	That's not fair.
FLUKE	What is fair around here?
VONIE	Well, will you not come up to the house for a bite to eat?
FLUKE	Will you come into my parlour, said the spider to the fly? Not I, not I. No way. No, no. 6 into 26 won't go.
VONIE	I'm only one.
FLUKE	Exactly. But what kind of one are you? What kind of ones are we? You don't know us. We don't know you. Leave it at that. Leave us apart. Close your parlour door.
VONIE	No.

Vonie exits. Fluke resumes the packing, helped by Laser.

LASER	Rocky, go over and give yourself a bit of a wash at the stream.
ROCKY	Why?
LASER	Clean the touch of that brute off yourself.
SCOTT	Will you make it over all right?
ROCKY	Sure. I've taken worse blows.
SCOTT	Do you want me to walk with you?
ROCKY	If you feel like a stroll.
SCOTT	Wouldn't mind.
ROCKY	Scott, that was a terrible thing I said earlier about your

da.

SCOTT	I know.
ROCKY	Why didn't you brain me?
SCOTT	Because I think you were looking for me to do that. I'm a Prod, Rocky. Remember? I never give Fenians what they deserve.
ROCKY	You're not as green as you're cabbage looking.
SCOTT	I'm not as orange as I'm cabbage looking.
ROCKY	Smart boy.
SCOTT	You're looking at him.
ROCKY	Couldn't keep up with you.
SCOTT	Try. Hold on, just until I pack up.

Rocky helps Scott to pack, handing over Scott's underpants.

ROCKY	Frame them. They can be a souvenir of your visit south.
SCOTT	One I can manage without. Throw them there. They might grow.
ROCKY	Throw them away? Where are you living, youngfella? Clothes cost good money. They don't grow on trees. No throwing away.
SCOTT	Then you hold on to them. Keep them for your first wrestling bout.
ROCKY	Can't wait that long to get into them. Look.

Rocky pulls the underpants on over his trousers and models them.

ROCKY	What do you think, lads?
LASER	You, Rocky, very you.
FLUKE	Definitely.
ROCKY	Yeah, I think so as well. Thanks, Scott. You're very good. I like these that much I'm not taking them off.
SCOTT	What? Rocky, you'll be arrested. If that policeman sees –
ROCKY	At least I'll go to jail contented.
SCOTT	What if your woman up there looks down?
ROCKY	We can do an exchange.
SCOTT	I won't walk with you dressed like that.
ROCKY	Well, I won't walk with you dressed like that either. Wait a minute, Scott. Think your ma's bad? Wait till you see what mine landed home with.

Rocky pulls from his rucksack a pair of brightly coloured polka-dotted underpants and throws them at Scott.

ROCKY   There you go. Fair exchange is no robbery. Let's see how they suit you.

SCOTT   No way, mate.

ROCKY   Why not?

SCOTT   I'm not wearing these clown's things.

ROCKY   Coward.

SCOTT   I'm no coward.

ROCKY   Then get them on you.

Fluke and Laser cheer.

SCOTT   Lay off. Rocky, I couldn't walk about like you. What if a stranger saw me. I'm too shy, man. You know me, Fluke, I –

FLUKE   So it's just shyness stopping you. O.K. we won't look. We'll all turn our backs. Pull them on and pull them off. Nobody will see. Will that content you, Rocky?

ROCKY   Dead on.

SCOTT   This is ridiculous.

ROCKY   Go, Scott. Nobody will look at you. We'll believe you. Backs turned, boys. Eyes covered.

FLUKE   No peeking.

ROCKY   We're waiting, Scott.

Scott miserably looks at the underpants, hesitates, pulls them rapidly on over his trousers, moves to take them off, waits.

ROCKY   Well? Are you decent? Can we look.

SCOTT   Look.

They turn around. Scott bursts out laughing.

ROCKY   Good man.

SCOTT   Now I see them on I think they're fair great. Thanks, Rocky.

ROCKY   Don't mention it, kid. Want a fight?

They shadow box.

ROCKY   In the blue corner the spotted southpaw.
SCOTT   And in the red corner the flowery fly-weight.
ROCKY   We're a right pair of clowns now, aren't we.
SCOTT   Me? I'm no clown. I wear my underpants over my trousers. Who else does that?
FLUKE   Is it a bird?
LASER   Is it a plane?
ROCKY   No.
ALL   It's Superman.

Fluke and Laser sing the Superman theme. Rocky and Scott fly.

ROCKY   Righting wrongs.
SCOTT   Doing good.
ROCKY   Crushing villains.
SCOTT   Strong and true.
ROCKY and SCOTT   Superman
ROCKY   To the river.
SCOTT   To the river.

Rocky and Scott exit, flying.

LASER   Rocky and Scott seem to have hit it off.
FLUKE   With enough time they'll be hitting each other. Blood-brothers.
LASER   Like us?
FLUKE   Can't stand the sight of blood.
LASER   It's great it happened though. At least one positive –
FLUKE   Laser, would you do me a favour?
LASER   Ask, partner.
FLUKE   Grow up. Do that, if you can. Where the hell do you think you are? Still stuck in the schoolyard settling all the fithts? You're out of there now. This is the big, bad world you're in. What do you think happened here less than five minutes ago? Your wee dream was shattered. Organise a big march. All on our own. Nobody behind us. Just Catholics and Protestants. There's more to this world than Catholics and Protestants. There's power. It

doesn't always wear a uniform, but it's all around us, and we have none of it. Power can push our like aside. It can stop us from doing what we want. That's just what happened. And did we fight back? No. We shut our mouths through fear. The same fear is at home. It will put a quick end to Rocky and Scott hitting it off. What will happen there? When they meet, they might nod at each other if nobody's looking. If they're brave, they'll say hello. If they're heroes, they might go together to a football match. If there's a miracle, they might play on the same side. But miracles don't happen in the north. Not in the world we live in. Scenes with your big policeman, that's our world, son. So go and shine your wee ray of light elsewhere. I'm not in the mood for it now.

LASER I agree we have to change the system that –

FLUKE We are the system. We have to change ourselves.

LASER Did we not try to do that with this march?

FLUKE Do what? Why did we take this on? Youthful enthusiasm? Deep compassion for our fellow man? A sense of positive duty to the suffering in faraway lands? Take your pick. They're all enough to make you sick when our own breed tears the lining out of each other at home.

LASER Like you're doing to me now.

FLUKE Don't worry. I won't be doing it much longer. I have a bit of bad news for you. I agreed to this mad march because I thought if I broke the news to you while we were together, you wouldn't think me a total hypocrite. This is the last time I'll be hanging about with you. The da's issued an ultimatum. I'm spending too much time with a Catholic. They're a bad influence. They lead you astray. He might pay lip service to equality but underneath he's like me. A black Protestant. Still, you have to forgive him. He has his reasons. He blames all his radical chat for what happened to the brother.

LASER Who?

FLUKE My brother. Stephen. Steve. Stevie. The funeral, kid, where we met. The one you're so fond of telling people about. The one Prod buried in your Catholic cemetery.

LASER Your brother?

FLUKE   Everybody's brother.

LASER   You never said.

FLUKE   You never asked. Why do you think I ventured that far
into enemy territory? Why do you think I always shut up
when you start on about our meeting at that funeral? My
simple, stupid brother, who changed sides and died. You
couldn't really know that. You didn't even know his
name. How could you know? I'd warned Scott well to
close his mouth. I wasn't part of a family group. Nobody
else went.

LASER   I did.

FLUKE   Thanks.

Fluke rapidly packs away the remaining objects.

LASER   Why didn't you cry for him?

Silence

LASER   Why don't you cry for him?

FLUKE   Cry for the dead? I'm too busy crying for the living.

Laser touches Fluke.

LASER   O.K.?

FLUKE   O.K.

LASER   Sure?

FLUKE   Yes.

LASER   You leave me? Never. You won't turn your back on me.
You can't.

FLUKE   How do you know?

LASER   A dickiebird told me. A very private dickiebird. Only I
can hear him. He talks a lot like you, only lower, nearly
always under his breath. You have to listen real hard to
know what's going on. Somebdy I'll let you hear him.

FLUKE   When?

LASER   A happier time.

FLUKE   A better place.

Fluke slowly offers Laser his hand. Laser takes it.

FLUKE   Everything all right?
LASER   Yes.
FLUKE   Call those two and we'll get moving.
LASER   Hold on.
FLUKE   What for?

Laser takes off his shoes and shakes the dust from them.

LASER   'And whosoever shall not receive you, shake off the dust of your feet.'
FLUKE   Very good. You're learning.
LASER   Am I?
FLUKE   Put them back on or I'll have you arrested.
LASER   Make me do it. Force me. Beat me.
FLUKE   Wait till I get you home, Fenian, then I won't be touched for doing it.
LASER   Protestant brute.
FLUKE   You love it, martyr.
LASER   Not that much.
FLUKE   Don't argue with your superiors, come on. (*shouts*) Hi, yous two, get a move on. We're heading.
LASER   Where to?
FLUKE   Where else?
LASER   Home?
FLUKE   Sweet home.

Fluke starts to wheel the barrow. Laser sings.

LASER   We're on the one road,
Sharing the one load,
We're on the road to God knows where.
We're on the one road,
Maybe the wrong road,
But we're together now, who cares?

Fluke punctuates the song's remainder with cries of 'RUBBISH, I hate that song.'

LASER   Northmen, southmen, comrades all,
Dublin, Belfast, Cork and Donegal,
We're on the one road, singing alone,
Singing a soldier's –

Fluke sings.

FLUKE   God save our gracious Queen,
God save, God save our Queen.
God save our Queen.
Send her victorious,
Render her glorious,
God save, God save, our Queen,
God save our Queen.

PRODUCTION STILLS

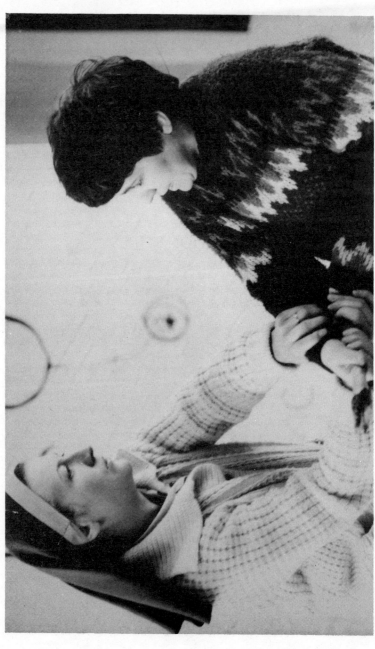

A scene from 'Jacko'. (Photo: Michael Foley).

'Borderlands' in Blackrock College.

'Then Moses Met Marconi'. (Photo: Michael Foley).

'*Then Moses Met Marconi*'. (Photo: *Michael Foley*).

A scene from 'Jacko'. (Photo: Michael Foley).

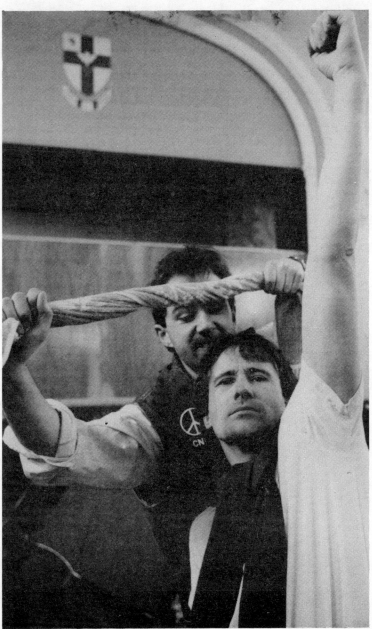

'Borderlands'.

A GENERAL NOTE ON WORKSHOPS

Each of the plays published in this volume was accompanied by a related drama-workshop when the programme was presented in schools. The aim of this workshop was to extend the educational experience beyond passive participation at a performance, and to offer a structure whereby the students with the actor-teachers could explore further the issues raised by the play.

With *Jacko* and *Moses* there was a performance for approximately two hundred students in the morning. The workshop was for between thirty and forty students and it lasted for between ninety minutes and two hours. We altered the format for *Borderlands*, presenting a two-hour programme twice a day to seventy students at a time. There was a performance for one hour and a quarter and a forty-five minute workshop for the entire audience. Time and numbers dictated that the *Borderlands* workshops were more formal and structured than their earlier counterparts for *Jacko* and *Moses*. While we regretted this increased structure, we also recognised that the play was better served by having a smaller audience and the workshops were at least available to everyone.

At the risk of simplification the workshops consisted of three distinct stages. The first involved the entire company playing with the students in a series of games and exercises designed to at once relax the students, create an atmosphere of trust, and focus concentration for the work ahead. We usually would begin with something loud and energetic and even deliberately silly and gradually work through games which demanded eye-contact, physical contact, concentration and spontaneity. We almost always used games rather than formal drama exercises because games by their nature discourage rational thinking and promote a spirit of enjoyable shared experiences. I have described some of these games in the notes relating to the specific plays.

What follows is a description of a few approaches taken in the case of each of the three plays in this book. It is impossible to adequately record the content of such workshops, and to try to do so would be a failure to recognise the value of the workshop process *per se*. It is the sense of shared problem-solving, the exchange of ideas and experiences on an equal basis, and the commitment to challenge the existing adopted positions on a whole range of issues, that most colours these sessions and that contributes to the students' sense of the workshops as significant educational experiences.

The workshop notes provided here are like maps, accurate and useful, but bearing little relationship in terms of scale or variety or colour to the infinite excitement of 'the real thing'.

JACKO WORKSHOPS

We often found that when we returned after lunch to take the workshop session the thirty students took some time to 'thaw out', and often defensively stuck with friends in the group rather than mingle at random. A good and simple game to encourage such uninhibited mixing is one we call: FIVE AT A TEA-PARTY.

The group comes out onto the floor and is asked to walk quickly around the space, covering the entire floor area, moving into open spaces, and all the time changing direction so as to avoid walking around in circles or along one axis only. When the group is thus involved the leader/actor-teacher periodically shouts instructions (or 'freeze' and then the instruction so as to have silence when giving the direction). (S)he may alternatively clap, whistle, bang a drum or tambourine to gain attention. The instructions are such as: 'Five at a tea-party'; 'Four in a jazz-band'; 'Six monks at prayer'; 'Three drunks going home'; 'Four kangaroos having a race' etc. etc. When the instruction is given everyone must find himself in a group of the correct number and perform the required activity until the instruction to 'Walk' is again given and the game resumes its pattern of alternate walking and activity. If it is the case that you eventually want to break the group of thirty into several smaller groups of five, six, or seven, then the game should finish with an instruction for that number. Thus you can arrive at random groups of the desired size without all the bother of counting and separating people.

Sometimes when the smaller groups were formed they went immediately into discussion out of which emerged the focus for the main part of their workshop activity. Often discussion about *Jacko* focussed sharply on the clash between Sr David and Andrew in the play. We usually extended beyond the particular to examine the fundamental tension between the needs of an institution and those of an individual. The notion of an institution was pursued to the point where sometimes lists were made of all the institutions in our society. Generally we attempted to focus on the institution with which we all had most contact: school. This could be done in many ways:

(i) MARY BROWNE AT SCHOOL
The group might split in two. Each half would draw or collage a life-size image of a thirteen year old student, name her, and establish a certain background for her. One group of four, as themselves and in accordance with their agreed vision of education, would list ten objectives for their student under the heading:

When she leaves school Mary Browne will:

    (i) . . . . .
    (ii) . . . . .
    (iii) . . . . .

The other half of the group as the principal, vice-principal, and two staff of the school we were in would simultaneously list their objectives for Mary Browne's period at school.

The two lists of objectives might then be compared and this would provide the meat of further work. For example the second group ('the staff') might have listed as an objective:

When she leaves school Mary Browne will be a strong and perfect Catholic.

The equivalent objective from the first group might have been:

When she leaves school Mary Browne will love God and her neighbour,
or such an objective might not have been mentioned at all. Within the clash of institutionalised schooling and individual young idealism therefore is hidden a tension between institutional religion and individual spirituality. This might well be the point for further discussions and improvisations.

It is important to emphasise at this point that in TEAM we distinguish clearly between *tension* and *conflict*. Too often, particularly with adolescents, improvised drama is concerned only with theatricalised conflicts: pregnant daughters; drunken fathers; and loutish school principals. This is to be eschewed. To be cultivated is the notion of tension, of depth of feeling, of internal wells of pride, insecurity and affection which are in fact the real sources of our actions. To return to the matter in hand as illustration. There is little to be gained from an improvisation between a mother screaming at her daughter that she must go to Mass and the daughter refusing to go with equal vehemence and lung-power. However with intelligent leadership from a teacher such an improvisation can have real value. It may be a question of taking the heat out of the situation by saying: *'Right, take it on a week or two after your row. The daughter is in the living-room reading. It is 4.30 on a Saturday afternoon and the mother and daughter are alone in the house. The mother decides it is a good time to talk to her daughter. She makes them both a cup of tea and enters.'* Now, at the risk of deflating the situation entirely, there is at least the basis for exploration. Note that I have not told the students that they are to avoid conflict, shouting and histrionics, because little is achieved by drawing their conscious attention to the problem. Rather, I have created a situation (late afternoon; they're alone in the house; reading and a cup of tea) in which exchange of ideas should be promoted. By making it Saturday afternoon, of which point they might need reminding, I have created an added tension in that the issue of going to Mass is tomorrow's reality.

It is obvious how such a situation, if it were proving fruitful, might provoke further improvisations that would extend the learning in many directions. For instance the group could explore the two parents discussing the matter; two or more parents from different families; the girl

and one of her friends; the parent and the class teacher or school principal.

All of this may seem a long way removed from *Jacko* but it has always
been our practice to structure the workshops from the raw material
thrown up in discussion and in the early exercises. In any case, although
I have wandered far from the specifics of child-care the fundamental
tension between personal freedom and institutional efficiency remains
constant.

No two workshops are ever the same. Consider for example how by
getting one of the initial groups to work on a profile of a male student
and a list of their educational objectives for him while the other half
does the same for a female student, you can shift the focus of the
workshop to the notion of sex-role stereotyping and sexism generally in
the curricula of Irish schools. This was an area of interest which we
explored in the *Moses* play and workshops.

(ii) THE ORANGE GAME

This refers to an exercise we used several times to bring home in a very
direct experiential way the notion in *Jacko* of people not really listening
to the other's point of view. Some of the company learned the game
initially at a business administration course, but it is important to understand why we felt it a useful exercise to do with students as we started
out on an afternoon's work on the play with them.

The idea of people not listening is at its most obvious in the scene
where Andrew goes to Joe in the discotheque but cannot penetrate the
loud music behind which Joe hides from his responsibilities, or put
otherwise, behind which he protects his privacy:

ANDREW: Look, could we go outside and talk?
    JOE   What?
ANDREW   Can we go outside?
    JOE   Yes. In a while. But there's this woman here; I don't want to
          miss her.
ANDREW   What?
    JOE   A woman. (*Moulds breasts on himself*) I'll be out later.
ANDREW   I can't wait.
    JOE   Then I'll see you in the morning.
ANDREW   It's no good in the morning. I'd want to see him first thing
          and be able to tell him something in the morning. You don't
          know what he's going through.
    JOE   What did you say? Will the morning do?
ANDREW   No, it won't do. (*Goes off. Joe goes off after his woman. High
          point in music cuts into a scream, high-pitched, from Jacko.*)

This notion of people not listening is fundamental to many relationships
in the play. Sr David feels Andrew does not really listen to her advice.
'*I'm tired talking*' she says at a certain point and despairs of bringing
Andrew to her point of view. Mrs Boyle's frustration with those in

authority is very much based on their 'Rathgar and Foxrock' way of listening or not listening to her 'Gardiner Street or Summerhill' way of talking: *'I was fool enough to think that I could make them understand'* she says, and when she's trying to describe her own feelings at one point she says: *'There isn't a name for it, because the people who make the names never lived where we lived'.* Her frustration with Andrew is matched in turn by his with the social-welfare official and his civil-service jargon.

The company had its own perverse illustration of this whole idea when we presented an extract from *Jacko* on *Anything Goes*, RTE Television's Saturday morning programme for young people. The extract was the one in which Mrs Boyle explains how her allowances were taken away from her and Andrew suggests that she get rid of the man she is living with so that her widow's allowance will be restored to her. *'How do you get rid of a man? Do you kill him? Tell him to fuck off?'* she spits back at Andrew. Immediately the 'phone lines in RTE were jammed with parents complaining about the bad language. There was not one call complaining about the far greater evil of the social welfare trap that Mrs Boyle and her like are forced into. It was a paradigm of one of the play's main themes: that people only listen to what they want to hear and make that their definition of normality and morality.

The Orange Game involved breaking the group of six or eight into two and talking to each group separately. Each half was told privately that they were a tribe who had shared access with the other tribe to an island on which grew a particular variety of oranges. This variety grew nowhere else. Tribe A were told that they used the oranges because the juice of this particular variety made them fertile and without the juice of 500 oranges once a year the whole tribe would stop reproducing and eventually die out. It was important not to over-emphasise that they only needed the juice as this might have alerted them to the solution. Tribe B were told that there was a chemical in the rind (again no undue emphasis on this point) of this variety of orange which reversed a fatal genetic disorder in their tribe. Without this chemical from the rind of 500 oranges once a year, they would eventually die out. Neither tribe wanted the other to know the reason why they needed the oranges as that would be to expose their weakness.

TRIBE A   ISLAND   TRIBE B

All was well as long as there was a good crop of oranges. However, one particular harvest yielded only 800 oranges. Anything less than 500 was no use to either tribe because it spelled death. The two tribes were asked to negotiate or elect representatives to negotiate with each other, bearing in mind all the points made above.

What this exercise explores is the process of communication. The solution to the dilemma should be obvious to the reader. All that has to happen is that the tribes agree to give the juice of the oranges to Tribe A and the rind to Tribe B. What often happens however is an exercise in non-communication, in distrust based on suspicion between the tribes, in status-seeking whereby positions are adopted and defended in a way that negates any possibility of shared understanding as a basis for a solution.

For the participants it is a marvellously direct experience of non-communication and there is a tangible shame and dismay when they are later told how simply they could have arrived at a solution ideal for both tribes. Time and time again (not always) each side comes away from the negotiations, convinced of the other's intransigence and their own reasonableness. Seldom enough does negotiation produce the solution that one half needs only the rind and the other the juice.

MOSES WORKSHOPS

PEOPLE TO PEOPLE
A very good opening game for a group of twenty-five or thirty is 'People to People'. It starts just like 'five at a Tea-party' described in the notes on the *Jacko* workshops. As the group walks around mingling, the leader/actor-teacher calls instructions like 'head to head' whereupon everyone has to quickly find a partner and they must make contact 'head to head' until the leader shouts 'Break!' and everyone resumes walking around until the next instruction which might be 'ear to ear', 'elbow to belly-button', 'bum to bum', 'hand to neck' or whatever. If there is an uneven number of participants – and the leader can control this by playing as well or staying out – the person left over is just abandoned for that turn, or the leader pairs off with the spare person, or the spare person becomes the new leader and calls the next instruction. The orders can be quite demanding e.g. 'knees to heels' and pairs may have to adopt strange contortions on the floor to achieve the required position. 'Eyelash to eyelash', 'hand to cheek' and similar instructions produce a closeness of contact which is sometimes to be sought after and sometimes to be eschewed. The game should be played with due sensitivity to this factor. One of the occupational hazards of allowing the students to become the leaders is that there is sometimes no limit to their sense of propriety or indeed to their sense of what is gymnastically possible!

THE CIRCLE NAME GAME
I mentioned in the general introduction to the workshops that we often played another game or two with the smaller groups of six or seven so as to build a good atmosphere and a sense of trust for the work to follow. In this context a game that we often used with students and which we use regularly in rehearsals, illustrates well the demands made upon players in terms of concentration and awareness. The specific linking of strong eye-contact with the use of people's first names made this an important game as we moved into working in smaller groups. It is a very difficult game, particularly so in boys' schools, but all the more rewarding for that when it succeeds. We call it 'The Circle Name Game'.

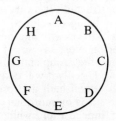

To start A, the leader, calls D by the first name. D walks in a straight line to take A's space. A 'to be rescued' makes strong eye-contact with another, e.g. F, and when F sees A looking at him calls A. A having been called by name now moves into F's space. F to be rescued looks at C. C calls F by name and then immediately looks for someone to rescue him as F is now advancing towards his space. G sees that C is looking at him and calls C by name. C moves to G. G looks at D. D calls G by name and looks to B. B calls G etc. etc. The game demands great concentration and to be played well should work at great speed with two or three people moving at the same time. To return to the sequence above for a moment: as D is still moving to A, A should have made contact with F who has called A so that A is already moving and F is now contacting C who calls him and *immediately* makes strong eye-contact with G. As soon as one player calls another's name, he then needs to be rescued and all other players should be looking to him to see if they are being sought as rescuers.

It is not an easy game to explain in theory, but a few 'trial and error' attempts will quickly reveal its difficulties and its excitements. Ultimately what makes the game work is the gradual 'tuning in' of the individual members to the group rhythm to the point where there is a collective energy generated and the group starts to respond as an entity. It is rare to achieve this immediately, though in my experience young people get there more quickly than adults. It is a game to come back to from time to time to increase expertise.

The notion of a collective energy and a shared understanding in a group is very important in drama work. It is both an end in itself and a stage in the process, a basis for further work. It is certainly a pre-requisite for the next exercise which I remember we first used when devising *Moses* in Annaghmakerrig, used again in rehearsals for the play, and also as a workshop exercise when touring the play in schools. It centres around character-work and indeed might well be called 'Building a Character' had not Stanislavski monopolised that phrase.

CONSTRUCTING A CHARACTER

A group of three or more (in workshops six) start with the notion of creating a character. Usually it begins with someone suggesting a name. Someone else responds to that name as it sounds to them or in terms of the image it presents. Then someone else adds another element and slowly the character is 'constructed'. It is very important that the group agrees with the character being developed. If someone suggests a feature of the character which jars with another's image of the character, then that second person must say so. If that happens then the character is abandoned and the group starts from scratch with a new name and builds from that. Usually it will take three or four attempts before some consensus is established, and provided no one is being deliberately unco-operative it is extraordinary the measure of agreement that can be achieved. Indeed after a while there is a vested interest in arriving at consensus so as to keep the character 'alive'. There is, in short, a group commitment to that character. This encourages the individual members to tune in to the collective intuition of the whole group. An example may be of help.

A B C D E F are in a group.

B: 'Laura is her name'
D: 'She's seventeen'
C: 'Blonde – long blonde hair'
F: 'She lives in an orphanage'

There is general disagreement with this and the exercise begins again:

A: 'Paul'
C: 'From Cork'
D: 'Yes, but living in Dublin'
B: 'Yes, an accountant, with a house in Rathmines'

F has seen Paul as a labourer or carpenter and cannot accommodate this notion of him as an accountant. He says so and Paul is left aside, and maybe this time or within the next few attempts which are getting longer each time, a consensus is arrived at and a fully rounded character is constructed.

In the *Moses* workshops this exercise was used to build a specific character: a seventeen-year-old schoolgirl. From this base a specific young woman was constructed by the group and was sometimes given a visual presence by a mixture of collage and drawing. I used to carry around envelopes full of eyes, ears, noses, mouths cut out from newspapers and magazines so that an image of the character could be established. Now the group of six had an identifiable character as a presence in the group. She became the focus for the rest of our afternoon's work.

I have often found that processes used in rehearsal prove very useful in workshop. In the early days of rehearsals for *Moses*, I had used string to establish the complex network of relationships operating in the play. The diagram below illustrates only one example of what I mean. Nuala, who entered up the hall of the school through the audience at the start of the play, was called home from Dublin by her widowed mother. As she returns, tugged home by this *umbilical cord*, she meets her former schoolfriend Joan Moore and starts to pick up the *threads* of her relationship with her. To stay in town however Nuala needs a job and she finds a *lifeline* thrown to her by Bobby Bold when he offers her a job in the radio station.

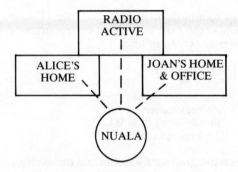

Nuala is the central character in the play because she has the most pieces of string/the most relationships. She is the most assured character because she manages, for the most part, to control the different pulls on her character without getting them entangled or herself tied up. I have deliberately chosen a particular idiom in which to write of the relationships because we went through the play in the early days of rehearsal with the actors having string rather than scripts in their hands, and eventually they found it a most useful and concrete way of entering the complexities of the play. Furthermore the terms 'cord', 'thread', 'line' are generally used in the context of relationships to give expression to the dynamic between people in any relationship, emphasising at once, as it were, their separation and their contact.

In workshops we attached five strings to our character to represent the different 'pulls' or influences under which she lived. These were categorised as in the diagram:

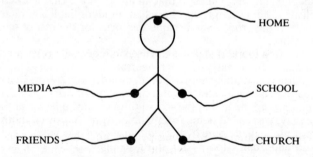

Within this structure there were many variables. Sometimes it was a question of finding an archetypal situation to represent the influence of home, or school, or friends, on the character and then this was improvised. Usually we attempted in the group to put the character under conflicting 'pulls' which is often the situation of a seventeen-year-old who has to try and accommodate how her friends think she should act with the expectations of her parents. It was never our intention to resolve such dilemmas, at least not simplistically, but rather to allow the students, through this surrogate character, establish the existence of such conflicting pulls and then explore how 'she' might resolve them.

WORKSHOP STRUCTURE

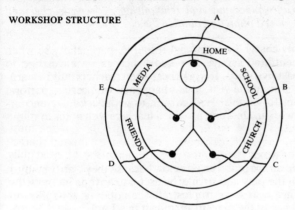

As the diagram above illustrates there is a structural relationship between this drama work where there is collective focussing of individual energies onto one character, and the earlier 'Circle Name Game'. This is not something to which the students' attention would be drawn however. It is merely the structural correlative of the need for a connection, albeit a sub-conscious one, between the initial games and exercises and the core activity of the workshop. It is something that I pursue later in the O'Grady sequence described in the section on the *Borderlands* workshops.

WORKSHOPS AND PASTORAL CARE

It is worth noting that there is an important 'confessional' element to TEAM's work in schools, particularly during the workshop sessions. The fact that the company is young, that it works hard at communicating openly with its audience onstage and off, that it presents work reflecting the interests of young people, and that the actors aren't around the next day to confront students with what they said in workshops, all combine to mean that students often see the workshops as an opportunity to express attitudes and feelings which would otherwise remain buried. Indeed in the TEAM office there is a file full of letters from students who write to the company about the plays they've seen and about their personal aspirations, and their thoughts and ideas on a range of topics and experiences. It is our practice to reply to each one of those letters.

In our 1984 submission to the Curriculum and Examinations Board, we wrote:

> *It is dangerous to make too many claims for theatre-in-education. Nothing can replace the vital relationship between teacher and pupil and indeed pupil and pupil in the classroom.*

T.I.E. is a highly-charged educational resource, particularly so when there is a concentrated service to schools such as we have tried to provide in the past five years. It works best when teachers build a learning programme around the visit, as has happened with certain pastoral care programmes to schools. With *Moses*, as with *Jacko*, we encouraged follow-up work in class and provided teachers with notes to stimulate such work.

MOSES FOLLOW-UP WORK
The notes for *Moses* are reproduced below because they clarify many of the intentions of the play and so may be useful to anyone interested in producing it. They also serve to illustrate the potential for follow-up work for a class seeing the play, or reading it in school.

Dear Teacher,
    TEAM Educational Theatre Company asks you to afford some time in class to follow up the impact of our visit to your school with this programme.
    Even a forty-minute period spent discussing the ideas raised by our visit will prove valuable.
    Our programme centres around *Then Moses Met Marconi*, a new play written by Bernard Farrell in collaboration with TEAM. Your attendance at the performance would, certainly, facilitate the best possible follow-up, but failing that, we have prepared a synopsis of the play, and a brief description of some of the ideas that we explore in it.
    Then Moses Met Marconi is set in a small pirate radio station 'somewhere in Ireland'. It centres around the lives of those who work in the station, and of some of those who listen. The disc jockeys are the super-confident Bobby Bold, the elegant Justin Day, and the enigmatic Wolfman Moses.
    They play the music and chat to the listeners, reminding them that Radio Active is their station – that it is 'the station that cares about *you*'. All is not as it seems, however: Bobby Bold is really Sean Delaney, and Justin Day is really Eamon McGovern – far from caring for its listeners, Radio Active is just another downbeat pirate station, established by the likes of Sean Delaney to make himself a fast buck.
    Delaney is anxious to boost his advertising revenue and his audience figures, to increase his chance of getting a local radio licence; when the play opens, he has decided that Radio Active needs a woman's voice to read the news and chat to the younger listeners.
    Nuala Ryan has just returned home from Dublin to spend some time

with her recently-widowed mother Alice. Nuala is a young, newly-qualified journalist, and Delaney chooses her for the job. Nuala believes the job will allow her the scope to realise the vast potential of community radio and at the same time she can continue in her efforts to restore her mother's self-confidence by encouraging her to take up again her old interests. Mrs Ryan at first resists these efforts, seeming content to play the role of the passive widow.

Returning to her home town has also brought Nuala into contact with an old friend from school, Joan, who is a secretary to the local solicitor, and engaged to be married. In the course of the play, we follow Nuala's activities in the radio station and in her private relationships with her mother and with Joan.

In both the public world and in her private life, Nuala is a critical force. Her own nature and her training have taught her to question many of the assumptions which underpin life in her home town. Her questioning unsettles her mother and Joan, and it increasingly unsettles the status-quo in the town. Just as she tries to liven up her mother by making her realise her full potential as a person, Nuala also makes the radio station truly *active*. With her magazine news programme, the station becomes a community forum for the discussion of ideas and issues of direct relevance to the people it serves.

For the first time in its broadcasting life, Radio Active begins to care for its listeners. Issues like schooling, land re-zoning, pub licensing and social-welfare payments are discussed. The powers-that-be begin to realise that Nuala Ryan and her magazine programme are a threat to their vested interests in the community. They believe in lip-service, while Nuala believes in the truth. When she is about to broadcast a programme on Women's Health, Sean Delaney comes under strong pressure to silence her.

On the private plane, Nuala's mother and Joan both seem affected by her ideas and her very presence that challenges them to examine their given social role as women. It seems doubtful whether Joan has sufficiently strong self-image to cope with all of this, but Mrs Ryan appears by the end of the play to be moving towards a greater sense of her own worth.

Through the medium of the radio station, and through the private lives of some of its listeners, Bernard Farrell explores the conventional masks we wear to avoid coming to terms with our real selves. *Then Moses Met Marconi* celebrates the need to unmask our true selves, and to communicate freely with one another – regardless of our age or sex, in private conversation and in the public media.

Then Moses Met Marconi is not an 'issue' play. It is not 'about' any one thing.

It is, rather, about how we deal with issues, in our public and in our private communication. The play draws on two main areas of expression:

The first is that of *the social role of women in our society*.

The second is that of how will we develop in Ireland a network of *local community radio stations.*

These two areas are not unrelated: radio has been an important force in the public education of Irish people about many different ideas, including the re-definition of the role of women in our society. At the same time, the re-definition of the role of women has been part of an exciting process of social education.

Our society must continue to examine the role of the media, if the organs of public communication are to be restored to the control of the communities they claim to serve. In 1983, we will be setting up, through our Deputies in the Dáil, the structures for local radio in the Eighties and Nineties. It is important that we make the right decisions.

By joining these two themes – women in our society, and local radio – Bernard Farrell's play is of particular importance to young people.

WOMAN
When we started devising this play with Bernard Farrell, we decided that the central character would be a woman. In TEAM's previous plays, we have been conscious that we have presented women as mere accessories to men – something that we share with most other theatre plays, and indeed which permeates our society in books, films, TV programmes, advertisements, and in the social and political structures of our country.

This play was about 'a person who happens to be a woman', and would avoid the tired clichés 'wives', 'widows', 'girlfriends', 'sisters', 'mothers', and the many other subsidiary roles in which women are usually cast.

Our play is not a sop to radical feminism. It simply *assumes* that it is normal, appropriate and entirely natural that the central character in a play can be both intelligent, humorous and imaginative, as well as a woman.

Suggestion 1: IMAGES OF WOMEN AS PORTRAYED IN THE MEDIA
Some students could collect advertisements from the newspapers and the magazines which portray women and men, both separately and together. Using these, a discussion could be started about the roles that women in advertisements are made to portray. Does the class think that there should be an advertising standard on this issue, as there is on the portrayal of violence, pornography and many other issues?

Suggestion 2: IMAGES OF WOMEN AS LEARNT AT SCHOOL
Can your students remember any of the stories from their primary school readers? Do these stories condition children's attitudes to male and female roles – 'little boys climb trees and get into scrapes, little girls help Mammy bake cakes and clean the house'? The class may decide to write a story for young people which would portray men and women as different and equal.

Suggestion 3: CURRICULUM DEVELOPMENT PLANNING

The class could be divided into several small groups – perhaps one all-male, one all-female, and one mixed if your school is co-educational. Each group could discuss the good and the bad points of the present school curriculum in the area of social/health/sex/relationships/education. From this, the students themselves could outline a course for fifth-year (pre-Leaving) students which would have one hour a week for 26 weeks.

Perhaps this could be sent to the Minister for Education for consideration?

RADIO

Some schools now have radio stations, run by their students.

- Does/would your school allow such a venture?
- What would be the editorial structure of such a radio?
- What does that say about the established roles of teacher and student?

Suggestion 1: COULD A NUMBER OF YOUR STUDENTS DRAW UP A MOCK PROGRAMME – PLAN FOR A SCHOOL RADIO STATION?

(a) What would be the editorial constraints upon the programmes' content?

(b) Divide the class into groups of five, and let half the groups decide on a list of the criteria that would apply in granting a local radio licence.

(c) They could then interview the other half of the groups, who have decided on the aims and policies of their radio station. Would the first group grant them licences?

Suggestion 2: COULD YOU GET A NUMBER OF YOUR STUDENTS TO DO A LIMITED SURVEY OF ONE WEEK'S LISTENING TO RTE/BBC/THE LOCAL 'PIRATE'?

They could ask their fellow-students, their parents and friends, and you, what programmes they listen to in one week. The results could then be correlated, and a programme schedule for one day's/one week's broadcasting by a local radio station could then be drawn up. It might be interesting to compare this to a copy of the RTE Guide!

Suggestion 3: COULD A FEW STUDENTS ARRANGE A LIVE INTERVIEW ('Vox Pop')?

Using an ordinary tape-recorder, some students could interview a friend, a teacher, another student, the local TD, etc., on an issue important to them.

What local issues do the students think should be discussed over the air?

Does your local station/RTE national network discuss such issues?

BORDERLANDS WORKSHOPS

FORMAT OF WORKSHOPS
The workshops for *Borderlands* were more structured because of the constraints of time and numbers alluded to in the general introduction to workshops. There was a more formal presentation of the workshops to the entire audience rather than a slower working-through certain processes between one actor-teacher and six or seven students as operated in the earlier programmes.

SOCIAL CONDITIONING
In the writing of *Borderlands* Frank had taken pains to place emphasis on the school and home experience of the four main characters. Their anecdotes about how they were brought up and in particular how they were schooled into certain attitudes and prejudices struck a chord with our school-going audience who were going through the same process themselves. The lines:

– *'What do they call religion in Protestant schools?'*
– *'History'*

never failed to raise a laugh. It was the laughter of recognition.

We explored this notion of social conditioning somewhat obtusely in workshops, and deliberately so. Too direct an approach would have alerted the students to the process and so prevented them responding spontaneously. We developed two strategies in particular, sometimes using them separately, sometimes in tandem.

(1) We worked with the students in an extended improvisation of a primary-school class learning to read. Page one of the reader went something like: THIS IS TOM; page two: THIS IS UNA; page three: THIS IS TOM AND DADDY; and page four: THIS IS UNA AND MAMMY. Page five went: TOM IS HELPING DADDY FIX THE CAR while page six was: UNA IS HELPING MAMMY IN THE HOUSE. We generally finished with page seven: UNA AND MAMMY ARE MAKING TEA FOR TOM AND DADDY.

This was a simple and enjoyable experience but the point was not lost on the students. They had re-experienced at an adult and conscious level what had been a child's sub-conscious conditioning about sex-roles. Ostensibly they had been learning to read which was a very laudable activity, but they had also been learning a whole set of not very laudable clichés about women's role in a patriarchal society. Part of our function as actor-teachers is not only to give the students certain experiences but also to provide them with the tools to deal with such experience. So we introduced them to the language of 'social conditioning'; of 'sex-role stereotyping'; of 'hidden curriculum' and of 'the social bias of language'.

(2) We read aloud several reports of deaths in Northern Ireland from
the most sketchy couple of lines through to a paragraph with an
amount of human-interest detail, and afterwards asked the
students to give a 'sympathy vote' on a scale of 1-10 to the person
killed. The pieces went like this:

THE IRISH TIMES, Jan. 17th 1974
LATE NEWS
A British soldier was killed late last night in South Armagh. He has
not yet been named.

IRISH PRESS, Oct. 2nd 1975
The British soldier killed last night outside Derry was named as
Corporal Michael Langley (18) of Aldershot.

THE IRISH TIMES, July 16th 1976
A young British soldier who had only been in Northern Ireland for
three days was killed yesterday morning in the Falls Road area of
Belfast. Lance Corporal Brian Trilling (22) from Berkshire was
married with two children.

RTE, Dec. 9th 1976
Police today identified the body of the British soldier killed last
night in Coleisland. He was Pvt. Paul Richards (21) of Bradford in
Yorkshire. Pvt. Richards had been returning from a party to celeb-
rate his 21st birthday when he was killed.

IRISH INDEPENDENT, March 30th 1978
The British soldier killed early yesterday morning outside Ennis-
killen was today named as Sgt. Peter Frayne (28). Sgt. Frayne was
due to return from his tour of duty in Northern Ireland next Satur-
day to join his wife who is expecting their first child. Mrs. Frayne
who is eight months pregnant was last night being comforted by
relatives at her parents home in Devon.

In fact all of these were fictitious pieces, carefully written to have an
increasing amount of emotional impact. Though we did not read them
out in the ascending order given above the students easily gave them an
appropriate rating according to the amount of information about the
victim that they had. We proposed to them that prejudice worked in an
equal but opposite way to sympathy, that prejudice in fact fed off lack
of knowledge, and those who wanted to perpetuate prejudice usually
deliberately cultivated ignorance or false images. In the absence of
truth the target for prejudice can be easily turned into a cliché and
therefore the perpetrators of sectarian prejudice, be that religious,
racial, or class prejudice have a vested interest in maintaining separatist
structures so that both parties never come to recognise their common
humanity.

Often such ideas developed into discussion about segregated school-ing and single-sex schooling, with reference back to the primary-school reader mentioned earlier, and to how the curriculum of Irish schools promotes certain social values above others, and expresses them as 'normal' or 'realistic'.

It is worthwhile perhaps to give an extended description of one BORDERLANDS workshop to demonstrate how it worked in practice. As usual it began with a game:

(i) IN THE RIVER ON THE BANK

Five or six students with two or three actors would line up facing the audience and the workshop leader. The leader tells them they are now 'on the bank'. If (s)he says 'in the river' they must immediately take a step forward. On the instruction 'on the bank' they take a step back. If already on the bank or in the river when told to move there they must not budge an inch or if you are playing really hard they must not even move a muscle. In short all they do is move a step forwards or back according to the instruction. The leader gives the instructions clearly and at a brisk pace. The complication is that the leader may call '*on* the river' or '*in* the bank'. Neither instruction should ever be obeyed, and should any player move for such a command (s)he is 'out'. The leader is the final arbiter and can obviously play the game as strictly as (s)he deems necessary.

This is one of the most simple yet enjoyable workshop games I know and we use it constantly. It can be played with large or small groups and it demands good concentration and self-discipline to play it well. There was always an added edge when it came to the last two or three players left, which often produced a good-humoured 'can the students beat the actors at their own game?' feeling. There were days, to our shame, when there wasn't an actor to be seen among the final half-dozen on the floor!

(ii) O'GRADY SAYS

A further six or eight students with two actors played 'O'Grady Says', again with the workshop leader in charge. This was also a high-spirited game with built-in opportunities for energy-release and for trust being established with instructions like: 'O'Grady says pull your left ear and laugh'.

Normally after 'In the River' and 'O'Grady' there was a good atmos-phere established and the relationship had changed from that existing in the performance part of the programme. The actor-teachers were by now dressed in their own clothes and sitting among the audience.

(iii) TRUST AND MISTRUST

The workshop leader declared that his name was O'Grady and proceeded to play the following improvisation with his daughter whom Linda, the actress who had played Vonie in BORDERLANDS, played. It was breakfast time. Mr O'Grady, already downstairs, is joined by his daughter whom we decided to call Linda for convenience. She notices that a letter addressed to her has been opened. Her father tells her that he opened it knowing it to be from Alan, whom he has forbidden her to see or have any dealings with . . . .

L: *You opened my letter. I don't believe it. After all you taught us about trust and privacy.*

O'G: *That's all very fine but if you proceed to abuse my trust, then I have no other option . . . .*

L: *How do you mean abuse?*

O'G: *I told you before that you were to have nothing to do with that fella.*

L: *You've never even met him. How can you . . . .*

O'G: *I don't need to meet him. I know his type.*

L: *Well, I don't care. I am going to continue seeing him.*

O'G: *Listen, young lady. As long as you live in this house you'll live by the rules of the house.*

The above is only the core of the improvisation. It was different every time it was played but the points about Mr O'Grady opening Linda's letter; O'Grady's prejudice and arrogance in the line 'I don't need to meet him, I know his type'; and the closed authoritarian logic (what I call the logic of 'O'Grady says') of O'Grady's last line above were always kept constant as they have a real bearing upon the play that went before and what was to follow in the remainder of the workshop.

For the moment the students were asked to retain the domestic O'Grady scene in their heads as we moved on to other matters.

(iv) STATUS CONTROL

From a pack of cards an Ace was produced and left in the middle of the 'field' where the play had been performed. If the Ace was taken to represent maximum status or control, the audience was asked to decide which of the four lads in the play held the Ace in their group. After some discussion it was generally agreed that Fluke did. Lorcan, who played Fluke, would then enter, pick up the Ace and, showing it to the audience, declare:

> 'I hold the Ace because of the four of us going to Dublin, I think that I understand my own situation best.'

The 'pattern' of the play was then followed when Linda who played Vonie, tried to take the Ace from Lorcan/Fluke, declaring:

'I hold the Ace because this is my land, my field and therefore what I say goes. However, I am not strong enough to force my authority, and therefore am going to call in the Guard.'

Peter, who played the Guard, would then enter and take the Ace from Fluke, declaring:

'I hold the Ace because I represent the authority of the State. I am a Garda Síochána, a Guardian of the Peace. I am here to implement the law of the land and that is why I hold the Ace.'

We then asked the audience where the Guard, whom we elected to call Guard O'Grady, got his authority and it was established that it was from the Minister for Justice.

(v) HIGHER AUTHORITY
There followed another short improvisation in which Vincent, our Production Manager, played the Minister for Justice, who was also called Mr O'Grady (!). He took the Ace from the Guard, and declared his authority and so his right to have the Ace. He then presented Peter/Guard O'Grady with his helmet in a formal way and addressed the audience as if it was the gathering of new Guards, their families and friends, at a passing-out parade in Templemore. His speech went:

'Guard O'Grady, I hereby invest you with the power and authority of the Garda Síochána. This is a difficult time for the Force which finds itself under attack not only from subversives but also from the so-called liberal press and the liberal sections of our society. I want you to be assured however that the silent majority of good, decent, hard-working people on this island totally supports your role as guardians of the peace, and protectors of the rights and property of individual citizens.'

(vi) WORKSHOP LEADER
The workshop leader would interrupt with something like:

'Well Minister, that was a clip from your recent speech in Templemore. With us in studio we have an invited audience who want to question you about a number of things or indeed to comment on what you have said.'

In this way we moved into open exchange between the students and the Minister and the Guard. The T.I.E. jargon for this is 'hot-seating' a character. The role of the TV interviewer afforded us a measure of control over this whole process and thus prevented the loquacious students from dominating the whole discussion. It also allowed us keep the discussion well focussed. The Criminal Justice Bill which was very *ad rem* at the time was a constant reference-point as was Section 31 of the Broadcasting Act. Indeed it was here that the relevance of the earlier domestic scene in which Mr O'Grady tore up his daughter's letter became obvious. The actor-teacher playing the Minister for Justice would continually defend the above legislation and if ever run to ground by particularly good questioning he would take refuge in the notion of the 'silent majority'. This last was a deliberate provocation, consciously allied to the play where the Guard justifies his actions to Vonie on the grounds that 'The silent majority is right behind us'.

(vii) THE SILENT MAJORITY
When the clock beat us as it invariably did, we concluded the session by reminding the students that they were part of the silent majority in which both Guard and Minister took refuge. We underlined the fact that it was impossible for them to say 'it doesn't affect me', to remain neutral because their silence was being invoked as tacit support. In other words 'O'Grady says *"The silent majority is right behind us".*' becomes a fact unless it is disproved.

As a final symbol of their need to take responsibility for the society in which they lived, we returned the Ace to centre-stage, in the field, surrounded by the students and visible to all of them. The Ace belonged to them, we suggested, and how they played it now and in the future would in part determine the nature of our society.

This particular workshop was deliberately provocative, and indeed on a number of occasions it provoked resentment from certain students who considered it subversive of the authority of the Guards. Most often this challenge was met from within the group of students themselves, with opposite positions being taken on issues like the Criminal Justice Bill and Section 31 of the Broadcasting Act.

BORDERLANDS and the accompanying workshops were intended to be provocative. Theatre-in-Education should not be 'agitational' or 'propagandist', we believe, but it should have the energy and commitment of agit-prop theatre. Above any specific idea or cause or 'ism', T.I.E. must be declaring to students that the shape and state of our society *matters*, and it must be challenging them to think about their contribution to that society. There is a dreadful stultifying hopelessness about many adolescents in the eighties, a feeling of 'it doesn't matter' which comes from an earlier feeling of 'there's nothing I can do'. By what we say and do TEAM proposes the value of making a contribution, of not accepting the existing model of the world for all time, and of finding the means within ourselves to build a better world. In touring our form of theatre-in-education from school to school and town to town, we are making a journey similar to that of Fluke, Laser, Scott and Rocky who push their wheelbarrow from Derry to Dublin in defiance of their parents' ancient animosities and for a cause bigger than the sum of their own inherited differences.

Before leaving the hall after the play and workshop we asked the students to bring their ideas and opinions back to the classroom and to find time there, in history or religion or civics or English class, to discuss

what they had seen and what they had felt. We gave them a poster/
programme both as souvenir and as stimulus. It contained three main
texts which attempted to define our responsibility as a theatre company
and their responsibility as an audience who were about to leave the
theatre and return to the 'real' world:

PROGRAMME NOTE BY TEAM THEATRE COMPANY

Fluke, Laser, Rocky and Scott make a march from Derry to Dublin. It
is also a journey from their inherited prejudices to some shared understanding in the present.

Fluke and Laser, at least, confront the myths of the past and the
images of the present which have been imposed upon them by school
and church and home. At the end of the play, they shake hands and
resolve to take responsibility for their future: *'We are the system. We
have to change ourselves'*.

BORDERLANDS is about the need to do your own thinking, and
about not automatically accepting the ideas and beliefs of a previous
generation. That need is as great for you – for all of us in the South – as
it is for the four lads from Derry.

The play was written for TEAM by a playwright who was born close
to Derry, both geographically and emotionally. It is his celebration of
how the young people of that city can rise above their parents' war. It
is also a warning and a plea to us in the South to listen to the people in
the North, and to stop responding in our own prejudiced, myth-ridden
way.

On leaving the theatre, you can either stop listening – like Vonie and
the Guard do – or you can continue to think and to talk and to listen
. . . and perhaps change.

PROGRAMME NOTE BY FRANK McGUINNESS

They say writers should do their talking through their writing. For a
playwright that is a fatal piece of advice. The characters in BORDER-
LANDS speak for themselves. I agree wholly with none of them. So
what was I doing in writing the play? When I try to answer that, I look
to a statement made by the great Irish historian, the late F. S. Lyons,
who said, *'To understand the past fully is to cease to live in it and to cease
to live in it is to take the earliest steps towards shaping what is to come
from the material of the present'*. BORDERLANDS is about responsibility, personal and political, and how the two are forever intertwined.

ON LEAVING THE THEATRE

Do not leave the theatre satisfied
Do not be reconciled

Have you been entertained?
Laughter that is not also an idea
Is cruel

Have you been touched?
Sympathy that's not also action
Corrodes

To make the play the writer used god's scissors
Whose was the pattern?
The actors rehearsed with care
Have they moulded you to their shape?
Has the lighting man blinded you
The designer dressed your ego?

You cannot live on our wax fruit
Leave the theatre hungry
For change.

Edward Bond.